SOMERSHAM HERITAGE

Alan Draper

All profits from the sale of this book will be donated to Charity

Published by Alan Draper

First Published 2014
© Alan Draper 2014

Printed and bound by
printmyownbook.com
St. Ives, Cambridgeshire

A catalogue record for this book
is available from The British Library
ISBN 978-0-9928565-0-2

Contents

Preface

There have been quite a few publications about Somersham and its history. The first may have been written by William Faux entitled "History of Somersham" which is reported in Pigot & Co's Directory of 1830 although I have not been able to locate a copy of it. In 1876 Nathan Dews, who was the village schoolmaster, also wrote a "History of Somersham". This was followed in 1890 by Charles E. Dawes who wrote a book titled "Somersham: Past and Present". There is a degree of overlap in the content of these two works.

In recent years John Bell (a former antique dealer in the village) and Andrew Lee (Historian and former Somersham resident) have each written a number of booklets about various aspects of Somersham's history. In 1995 Barbara Hoy (Somersham resident) wrote a booklet "Somersham, Historical Village of the Fen Uplands".

I moved to Somersham in 2006 and the following year became a member of the Parochial Church Council of St John the Baptist Parish Church. I soon found myself taking on the task of organising a heritage exhibition in the Church which proved to be very popular with many people in the village and beyond. Later I helped to form, and became Chairman of, an organisation called 'Friends of Somersham Parish Church' (FSPC). The 'Friends' comprises of people who have an interest in, or an attachment to, this Grade I historic building and the churchyard, but who may not necessarily wish to be part of the congregation or indeed worship regularly at the church. As part of the fundraising side of FSPC I organised a second heritage exhibition, which again proved to be very popular and raised a good deal of money to put towards the improvements in the church that were carried out in 2013. A third, equally popular, exhibition followed in September 2013.

The three exhibitions involved me in a lot of research and although I had the former publications to support my work I was saddened to find little of the 20th century village history recorded.

It has been my intention in this book to combine a summary of some of the previous accounts of Somersham's history with 19th, and principally, 20th century developments in the village and even look at some events in the 21st century. I hope that readers will discover some interesting and fascinating information about Somersham of which they were not previously aware.

Acknowledgements

I would like to thank my wife Jean for all the help and encouragement she has given me with the research for this book and the three Heritage Exhibitions. I am very grateful to her for proof reading the text and giving me advice on the content and format of this book.

A number of people have allowed me to use their research and writings and therefore made some important input: Jerome Bertram for the information he supplied about the SOE; David Collingswood for his contribution about the Dovecote; Steve Criswell for his help with the information about farming; Julyan Hunter for the research about 'Schools and Education'; Wendy Roberts for the research into the Somersham Chemists; Ron Newson for the information about the work of the Feoffees Charity; Dave Ruddlesden for his work on the trade directories; Cedric Williams for the research into the Old Rectory; Tom Busby for material about Somersham from his autobiography; Barbara Hoy for allowing me to use material from her book and the sports clubs and other village organisations for their own contributions. I am also very grateful to all the people who have allowed me to scan their photographs and postcards, some of which I have used in this book and have helped me to acquire a wealth of pictorial material for use in the exhibitions. I am thankful to the many people in Somersham who have provided me with much relevant information, either when I have interviewed them, or just in casual conversation. They know who they are, there are too many to mention and I am fearful that if I did attempt to list them I might offend any that I had omitted to include.

I am grateful to Andy Lee who helped me with some of the historical information for the first Heritage Exhibition. Also to

Penny Bryant (Clerk to Somersham Parish Council), the staff at Huntingdonshire Archives and Local Studies and the Curator of the Norris Museum (St. Ives) who enabled me to access records in their care. Age Exchange have allowed me to use the information in their publication 'Goodnight Children Everywhere' about Jim Brittain.

Finally I would like to thank Claire Callan who proof read my finished book very thoroughly and made many helpful suggestions which I have adopted.

Photographic Acknowledgments
Huntingdonshire Archives and Local Studies have granted permission to use photographs of the following two maps:
2196/37A—Somersham Tithe Map, 1838 and
Map 39—George Thomson's Estate Map, 1819

SSM 11.F Parkhall Estate, Somersham - Copyright to the Francis Frith Collection.

Other photographs are either now out of copyright or the owners have allowed me to scan and use them. The remaining photographs were taken by me.

INTRODUCTION

Somersham lies on the edge of the Fens and is believed to have been covered in part by dense forests and was fairly marshy and partly surrounded by water. Various remains from Roman times and before have been found in the parish.

At first sight Somersham does not appear to be very different from many other villages in Cambridgeshire until you start to delve into its history.

The village also appears to have been a place of note in Anglo-Saxon times as it was the residence of one of the early lords of the county. A nobleman called Britnoth (or Brithnoth) gave it to the Monastery of Ely in 991 AD.

In the Domesday Book, compiled for William the Conqueror in 1086, the description given of the village seems to indicate that Somersham was in a very prosperous condition. It is called "Summersham", which historians say is probably a Saxon interpretation of a summer station of the Romans.

Somersham was a market town having been granted a Royal Charter in 1190 in the reign of Richard I which gave the Bishop of Ely the right to hold a weekly Thursday market. The charter was reaffirmed in 1199 by King John, but since the beginning of the 19th century the market has been discontinued. There were also two annual fairs one held on 24th June, the patronal festival of St John the Baptist, to whom the village church is dedicated, and the other on the Friday before 22nd November.

Somersham was the site of a Palace belonging to the Bishops of Ely and the surrounding woodland formed part of the royal forests which were cut down early in the 14th century. At least four kings of England visited the Palace to hunt.

In the 14th century the Bishops of Ely had a number of different residences including a Palace at Somersham. There is no record of when it was built, although it is thought to have been in the 12th century.

Somersham was formerly on the old coaching route from St. Ives to Wisbech. The village consisted for many years principally of one road (High Street) about three quarters of a mile long running east west which is crossed by a second road near the centre. However, the St. Ives Road curves in a north easterly direction in a broad arc before curving back east and joining the High Street. It is thought that at one time the St. Ives Road was fairly straight and ran into Pinfold Lane, therefore passing south of the church and putting that building at the centre of the village. A number of arguments have been put forward to

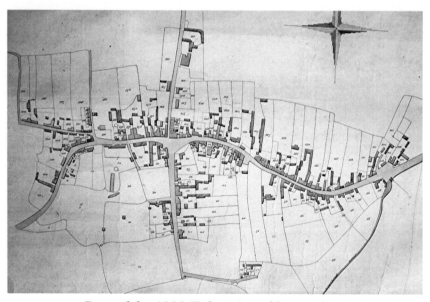

Part of the 1838 Tithe Map of Somersham

support this theory and these are explored in a paper by C.C. Taylor in the book 'Cornwall to Caithness: Some aspects of Field Archaeology'. Today the village has many roads, some of which have come about by the building of various housing developments in the second half of the 20th century.

Somersham once had a railway station connecting it to the towns of March and St. Ives as well as a short branch line to Ramsey.

In Anglo-Saxon times Huntingdonshire was a county that was divided for administrative purposes into districts called hundreds plus the Borough of Huntingdon. Each hundred had a separate council that met each month to rule on local judicial and taxation matters. The Parish of Somersham was part of the Hurstingstone Hundred.

Somersham Parish Council came into existence in 1894 as a result of the Local Government Act of that year. Its first meeting was held on Tuesday 4th December. However, the wider administration of the area was under the control of the St. Ives Rural District Council of which Somersham was the second largest village after Warboys. The RDC had control of local housing and there is a plaque on the front of 28 High Street which notes that it was built in 1960 and was the 1,000th Council House built by St. Ives RDC. Four years later the Lord Lieutenant of the County, Lord de Ramsey, opened the Windsor Court flats for elderly people, the first scheme of its kind in the County.

The 1974 Local Government Act saw the end of the RDC and the County of Huntingdonshire (England's third smallest county after Rutland and Middlesex) was amalgamated with Cambridge, Peterborough and the Isle of Ely to become the new Cambridgeshire County Council. The old county became a district of the County Council originally being called Huntingdon District Council and in 1984 changing its name to Huntingdonshire District Council.

Somersham is sometimes referred to as a 'Town' a term which obviously comes from its medieval charter and the right to have a weekly market. 'Town' is still retained by the main sports clubs and the brass band, yet by nature of its size and importance in the county, let alone the country, Somersham is referred to as a village. Even today some of the older inhabitants talk about the town and 'townsfolk'.

The Meridian Line Marker outside No 91 High Street,

There is one other thing that is worth noting about Somersham, it is that the Prime (Greenwich) Meridian passes through the centre of the village. Apparently there are only a few places in England where this actually occurs. The Greenwich Meridian separates east from west in the same way that the Equator separates north from south. Inextricably linked with Greenwich Mean Time, it also sits at the centre of our system of time zones. Just as the meridian line is marked at Greenwich by a metal bar on the ground, so in Somersham it is marked by two brass bars set in the pavement on either side of the High Street close to the 'Cross' at the centre of the village.

THE POPULATION

The first indication of the number of people living in Somersham comes in the Domesday Book which was a survey of England carried out for William the Conqueror around **1086 AD**. Somersham was recorded as having **32 villagers**. However, that figure might only relate to the number of men in the village.

The next record is a list of the **70 villagers** of Somersham who were taxed by Edward III in **1327/28**. This list of names appears to only include men, so the actual population of the village would have been greater as women and children need to be added to this figure.

The Protestation Return of **1641** for Somersham, which was a form of oath by which individuals undertook to defend the kingdom, the crown and "the true reformed protestant religion" has **157 names** recorded for Somersham, but the returns are only of males over the age of 18.

The Hearth Tax returns of **1674** give **104 names**, mostly men, but a number of widows. This tax was introduced in 1662, 'it being easy to tell the number of hearths, which remove not as heads or polls do'. So the figure is probably better considered as the number of households in the village. However, hearth tax returns have been used to estimate population. It has been argued that the average household size, in both rural and urban areas, outside London was 4.3. Clearly, precise figures cannot be obtained, but on this basis the population of Somersham would have been 447.

It is interesting to compare these figures with the **1801** Census which gives the population of Somersham as **833**, this includes men and women. However, it is generally acknowledged that in the early censuses (1801, 1811, 1821 & 1831) there was a fair degree of under-recording.

In the following table I have taken the liberty of using the 4.3 multiplier to calculate corrected figures for the population.

Source	Year	Number given	Corrected Figure
Domesday Book	1086	32 "villagers" (may have only been men)	137
Tax Return (Edward III)	1327/8	70 men	301
Protestation Returns	1641	157 males over 18	675
Hearth Tax	1674	104 mostly men	447
First National Census	1801	833 individuals	833

The 1801 census asked local officials to provide information on the number of inhabited and uninhabited houses in the parish and how many families occupied them; the number of people in the

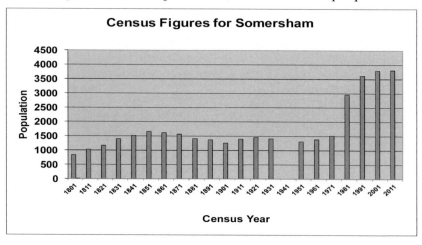

parish and their employment; and numbers of baptisms, burials and marriages in the previous 100 years. A similar format was followed for the censuses of 1811, 1821 and 1831, with the addition of further questions. Most of the early returns for 1801-1831 were destroyed, only statistical summaries being published.

Year	Men	Women	Population	Pop. Increase	% Increase
1801	393	440	833		
1811	493	539	1032	199	23.89
1821	562	604	1166	134	12.98
1831	725	677	1402	236	20.24
1841	766	751	1517	115	8.20
1851	832	821	1653	136	8.97
1861	784	837	1621	-32	-1.94
1871	762	800	1562	-59	-3.64
1881	692	717	1409	-153	-9.80
1891	714	667	1381	-28	-1.99
1901	635	620	1255	-126	-9.12
1911	728	676	1404	149	11.87
1921	727	739	1466	62	4.42
1931	706	711	1417	-49	-3.34
1941					
1951	640	677	1317	-100	-7.06
1961	678	713	1391	74	5.62
1971	751	762	1513	122	8.77
1981	1470	1501	2971	1458	96.36
1991	1796	1821	3617	646	21.74
2001	1878	1924	3802	185	5.11
2011	1902	1908	3810	8	0.21

The table above shows the basic census statistics for Somersham from 1801 until 2011.

The most noticeable increase in Somersham's population was between 1971 and 1981 when the new housing in and around The Trundle and in and around Grange Road was built. However, you will notice that the population of the village also decreased particularly between 1861 and 1901.

In 1890 Charles E. Dawes in his book 'Somersham Past and Present' wrote:

"It is disappointing to have to chronicle nothing but diminution in the size of the village, decreased prosperity of its inhabitants, and a general state of affairs at a lower level than in previous centuries; but nevertheless, such is the case, and Somersham is not alone in this particular, it having only experienced the vicissitudes common to all agricultural communities. Various causes have conspired to bring about this state of things. Its people have migrated to centres where there is more scope for their abilities, with the intention of improving their condition, and the consequence is that whilst the manufacturing districts, where work is fairly plentiful, are congested, those purely agricultural are comparatively deserted, and have to bear the brunt of the general depression. Another cause is the depreciated value of land. Land bought years ago for £90 and £100 per acre, if put to the hammer to-day, could not be sold for half that amount.

The only change for the better, which succeeding centuries have produced, is the alteration in the appearance of the village. The collection of rude huts has given place to the rows of well-built houses which may now be seen when passing through the village. This change has been brought about to a great extent by the altered social condition of the people, who are no longer feudal serfs, but free men, able to think and act for themselves. The houses of the last century were for the greater part whitewashed on the outside, and it has been remarked that the

18

village had an air of neatness and cleanliness seldom seen. A few cottages of this character with thatched roofs still remain, but most of the dwelling-houses are now built of brick and tile, or brick and slate. In spite of the change Somersham has still the reputation of being one of the cleanest and neatest villages in the county."

The village was awarded the county trophy as 'Best Kept Village' in 1967. A tree planted in the churchyard, complete with plaque to commemorate the occasion can still be seen today.

MAPS

One of the earliest maps that showed Somersham was one of the County of Huntingdon drawn by Eman Bowen (Geographer to the King) in 1560 for Robert Montagu, Duke of Manchester. *A colour copy of this can be purchased from the Huntingdonshire Archives.* It shows the main roads in the village, some small illustrations of buildings that indicate the approximate positions of the Bishop's Palace, the Church and the Manor Hall and the names of Hammond Esq. and Thompson Junr. Esq. Other very old maps of the County show **Trundle Wood** just to the west of Somersham.

The oldest surviving map that shows details of the village is dated 1819 and is a plan of an estate partly in the Parish of Colne and partly in the Parish of Somersham, the Property of George Thomson Esq. It is an area that we know today as **Colnefields** and part of **The Bank.**

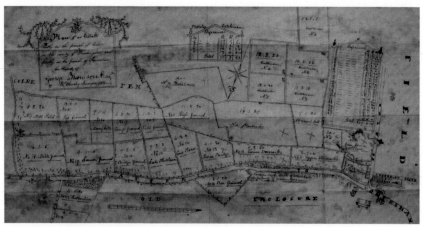

Map of George Thomson's Estate—dated 1819

The first really detailed map of Somersham is the **1838 Tithe Map**. It is subdivided into numbered plots of property and land

21

and the accompanying index lists the names of owners and occupants of each one. It is very large and in pastel colours and kept rolled up. *It is necessary to make an appointment to see it at the Huntingdonshire Archives as it needs to be spread over several large tables.*

The **1887 Ordnance Survey Map** of the village is the oldest one kept at Huntingdonshire Archives. It is the first one to show the station and the railway and it is interesting to note that the section of Parkhall Road, then called Squires Lane, north of the Manor Hall up to the railway bridge is mainly lined with trees and has only one property on it, Drove House, marked B.H. (Beer House).

The next Ordnance Survey Map of the village, also kept at Huntingdonshire Archives, is dated 1924. Most of the buildings on the map are the same as on the previous one but there are now more houses in Parkhall Road. On the west side of the road is the short terrace named Willingham Buildings and on the other side of the road are a number of separate houses, which according to the current owners, were built around 1910 or slightly later. To the east of the railway line the houses in Bank Avenue appear on a map for the first time. There are a few isolated houses on the St. Ives Road which still exist today. In the High Street a building is labelled *'Picture Theatre'* it was later known as *'The Palace'*. This building is now used by the Royal British Legion and the Centurion Club.

Sadly Huntingdonshire Archives collection of large 1950s Ordnance Survey maps is incomplete and only the sections of Somersham that show the southern part of the village are present. However, a privately owned One-Inch Ordnance Survey Map (1950 edition) shows the addition of Coronation Avenue and Norwood Road but no indication of Feoffees Road.

THE MANOR

The first recorded Lord of the Manor of Somersham was Britnoth, or Brithnoth, Duke of Northumbria, who gave this and several other valuable manors to the Monastery of Ely on condition that if he should be slain in battle, the monks should inter his body in their church. In 991 Brithnoth was killed by the Danes at the Battle of Maldon and his body, minus its head which the Danes had cut off, was brought back to Ely and interred in the monk's 10th century Saxon church.

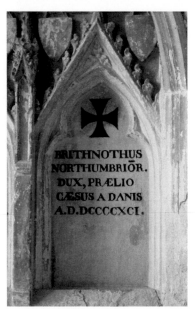

Brithnoth's tomb in Ely Cathedral.

The translated inscription reads "Brithnoth, Duke of Northumberland, killed in battle" by the Danes 991 AD.

The headless skeleton of Brithnoth was moved to the present Cathedral by 1154. It has been moved several times but the tomb shown here is situated in Bishop West's Chapel at the eastern end of the Cathedral's South aisle.

The Abbey at Ely then, as agreed, became the owner of the Manor of Somersham which was let out to tenants who, in lieu of rent, were obliged to send in provisions for a certain period of the year. "Sumersham" had to furnish provisions for two weeks in the year, and Bluntisham and Colne one week each.

Somersham acquired its first charter under Richard I, a King who (contrary to what has been suggested) is not likely to have visited the village, spending most of his reign out of the country. However, the Bishop of Ely, William Longchamps certainly did and as he was Lord Chancellor for much of the early part of Richard's reign, ruling the country in the King's absence, it was probably through his direct influence that Somersham acquired the charter.

This would not have been an act of generosity by the Bishop for his tenants. As the village crops increased and people had more than they needed, they wanted the chance to trade their surplus. Without a market the Bishop was the only man in the manor who could have bought the surpluses, and as his own farming enterprises also had surpluses, he had no need of the peasant's grain. However by setting up a market and encouraging traders in from outside, he offered an opportunity for his tenant farmers to trade and he could take a percentage of all the goods that were bought and sold there.

In 1199 it appears that King John either granted a new charter to the Bishop of Ely, or renewed the former one giving him full possession of the manor, market, lands and wood of 'Sumersham'. In 1229 Henry III renewed the charter granting 'Somersham Forest' to the Bishop of Ely. At the end of the Norman era much of the land around Somersham was still covered by forests. During the Middle Ages this was gradually cleared to provide grazing land. By the time of the Tudors much of it was described as 'The Chace', open park land for deer.

Throughout the Middle Ages most of the land in and around Somersham was held by the Lord of the Manor, the Bishop of Ely. The Soke of Somersham included Bluntisham, Colne and Pidley-cum-Fenton. The Church was a powerful land owner across England and throughout the 16th century there were continual attempts by the Crown and others to obtain possession

24

of Somersham. It was not, however, until 1600 that Bishop Heaton exchanged the Manor and Soke, valued at £1,132 3*s*. 9¼*d*. yearly, with the Crown for property valued at £1,144 19*s*. 7½*d*.

The village remained the property of the Crown until 1620 when the Manor and Soke was leased for 99 years, by James I to Henry Jermyn, later the Earl of St. Albans. The Earl, along with others, acted as a trustee for the benefit of his son Charles who became Charles I. The Manor then became part of the jointure of his Queen, Henrietta Maria.

In 1641 Somersham figured in the great divide that split Oliver Cromwell from the Parliament of that day. The Duke of Manchester, as tenant of the Queen's Palace of Somersham, had enclosed much of the common heath land around the Palace that the villagers were accustomed to use for grazing their cattle. The villagers rioted and tore down the enclosures and gained the support of Cromwell who had 'in great fury' attacked the King's Court for its dealings on a petition of some of his constituents from Old Huntingdonshire. He reproached the Chairman for being partial in his decision. An historian stated 'Having tracked this matter by faint indication, I conclude that the petition related to the Soke of Somersham'. Cromwell knew the Soke of Somersham very well and knew about the people and the treatment that they received. In time, along with other matters, this sort of grievance led to the Civil War of 1642.

During the Civil War, the Palace, Park and Chace were granted to Colonel Walton, the brother-in-law of Oliver Cromwell, 'in satisfaction for £2,132. 6s. due to him for monies advanced for the use of the Commonwealth'. The grant bears the date November 1649. Charles Dawes wrote *'we are told that Colonel Walton very much improved Somersham by erecting decoys etc, but immediately before the Restoration (on the eve of which he had retired to the Continent), the common people, to express their dislike to him, broke in and totally destroyed them'.* He went on to explain that the decoys were used for the capture of various kinds of aquatic wild-fowl, principally wild ducks.

When the country returned to being a monarchy the remainder of the lease of Somersham was given back to the Queen Dowager, Henrietta Maria. Her trustees in 1661 leased the Manor and Soke for 21 years to Charles Cornwallis who in 1663 obtained a further term of 21 years. Henrietta Maria died in 1669, and in 1672 the residue of the 99 year lease was granted to trustees for the jointure of Catherine, Queen of Charles II, to whom in the following year an additional term of 43 years was granted.

In 1673 the reversion in fee of the Manor and Soke was granted to George Viscount Grandison and Edward Villiers to be held of the manor of East Greenwich in free and common socage. (A form of feudal tenure in which land was held not by service but by a money rent). These grantees sold their interest in 1675 to Anthony Hammond of St. Albans Court, Nonington (Co. Kent). The Hammonds of Kent then became Lords of the Soke of Somersham.

By 1680 Thomas Thompson (brother-in-law of Anthony Hammond) and his family were living at the Manor Hall and were generally called the "Squires" of the village. Hence the lane in which the house stands was called Squires Lane. It is now called Parkhall Road, probably because it leads to Park Hall, a building at the northern end of the road. Today a plaque on the Manor Hall (Numbers 21 & 23 Parkhall Road) declares that Squire Thompson rebuilt the house in about 1720. The Thompsons lived in Somersham for many years after the last of the Hammond's (Thomas) died. William Thompson was High

Sheriff of Huntingdonshire and Cambridgeshire in 1733 and George Thompson held the same office in 1824.

The Soke of Somersham remained in the possession of the Hammond family until it was sold to the Duke of Manchester by Thomas Hammond, who left no children. The park was enclosed and divided into farms.

At the inclosure of Somersham Heath in 1796, the Manor was no longer held by the Duke of Manchester, but along with the Soke it was in the hands of Sir Robert Burton of Woodhurst. One twentieth of the waste ground within the Manors of Somersham and Pidley was allotted to him in lieu of this claim to the waste as Lord of those Manors. The manorial rights were in the possession of John Ansley in 1814 and of George Ranking and Joseph Burkett Jackson in 1815. They were put up for sale in 1816 and were held by Mr. John Guillum Scott, High Sheriff, in 1830. They were owned by James Cudden of Wimpole Street, London in 1860, who enfranchised much of the land. By 1869 the Lord of the Manor was John Garrard Elgood, of Lincoln's Inn Fields, London. He was succeeded before 1906 by W. A. Elgood. Unfortunately I have not been able to find the present owner.

THE BISHOP'S PALACE

The Bishopric of Ely was created in 1109 and Somersham became a part of the endowment. From the 12th century the Palace became an Episcopal residence of some importance being relatively close to Ely and at the end of the first stage of most journeys made by the Bishops of Ely on their way to London.

About this time the Bishop created elaborate gardens around his Palace, built of Barnack stone. There were two lakes supporting duck, swan and heron on either side of the approach to the building. To the side of the Palace there were small enclosed gardens surrounded by a moat. Behind the Palace further gardens lay either side of a raised causeway, known as Lady's Walk with views across various parts of the garden. Ornamental fish ponds, a terraced walk, water garden and an orchard were all part of the Palace. Only the moat and fish ponds remain of the original Palace structure or its former glory. The wall of narrow red brick, which is still in existence, is said to be 16th century.

The repairs to the house and the wages for a gardener tell us that the Bishop's Palace can trace its origins at least as far back as 1169, if not earlier. It became a very popular country seat for many of the medieval bishops and there was a splendid forest where bishops and their guests could hunt. In 1197 Bishop Eustachius, the fifth Bishop of Ely, had the hunting of the big woods granted to him by Richard I. The bishops were able to hunt deer in the forest until 1762.

Bishop Hugh de Northwold was in residence at the Palace in 1228 and he set about improving the structure of the church.

Bishop John Hotham came to Somersham in 1316, but did not consider the property worthy of his rank, let alone that of visiting royalty and arranged for a palace 'fit for a king' to be constructed near to the site of the first Palace. In 1319 King Edward II granted the right to hold a fair on the vigil and feast day of the Nativity of St. John the Baptist and the two following days June 23rd – 26th.

In 1520 Bishop Nicholas West described the Palace as 'his poor home of Somersham'. In a letter to Cardinal Wolsey he said that he could not leave the Palace and no one could come to him without great danger, except by boat. However, the Palace must have been quite imposing, being enlarged from time to time and particularly during the reign of King Henry VIII by Bishop James Stanley, a son of the Earl of Derby. The Tudor walls of a walled garden and the farm courtyard remain.

The Palace was one of the three places suggested in 1533 as a suitable residence for Queen Catherine of Aragon, then divorced from Henry VIII. This was vigorously opposed by the Spanish Ambassador and the plan was dropped. Queen Catherine went instead to Buckden.

In 1535 Bishop Goodrich sent out from the Palace a mandate to his clergy. This was to command them to delete the name of the Pope from their books, and to publish to all the churches of the diocese of Ely that the Pope no longer had any authority in the Kingdom. Bishop Goodrich died at Somersham in 1554 and was succeeded by Thomas Thirlby. He was deprived by Queen Elizabeth I because he was Roman Catholic and she appointed Richard Cox in 1559, the first Protestant Bishop of Ely. He was the last Bishop to live at the Palace.

Bishop Cox resigned in 1581 and from this time the fortunes of the Palace took a downward turn. No one was appointed to succeed him until 1600 and during this time Queen Elizabeth I took the revenue from the estate.

In 1588 it was proposed to make the Palace a place of confinement for recusants (Roman Catholics who refused to attend the services of the Church of England) and a survey was made of the estate. The building was in a very sad condition with much lead, timber and glass missing. Sir John Cutts, the keeper of the Chace, was ordered to make it ready for the Huntingdonshire recusants in 1594, but although repairs were probably made there is no record to prove that it was actually used for this purpose.

In 1604 the Palace was visited by King James I *(see: Royal Visitors to Somersham)*. Then in 1611 Thomas, Earl of Suffolk, was appointed as keeper of the Palace and bailiff of the Manor and Soke of Somersham and he resided there until 1630.

King Charles I leased the Palace from 1636 until 1641 and passed it on to his French Queen Henrietta Maria. It was administered by her trustees who were empowered to grant leases for periods of up to 21 years.

Over the years leases were granted to various individuals and in 1653 the property was even put up for sale by the trustees. The site of the Palace covered 10 acres and was surrounded by a moat and it is thought that it must have fallen into disrepair as the value of the courthouse, over and above a charge for demolition, was valued at £320.

Eventually it passed to the Hammonds when they became Lords of the Soke of Somersham in 1675. Anthony Hammond came to live in one wing of the Palace with Thomas Thompson, who had married Anthony's sister Pheobe. Anthony died in 1680 at the age of 39 years and a black and white monument to his memory was erected on the north wall of the Parish Church. Hammond's son and heir, also named Anthony and aged 13, inherited the property and allowed the buildings to fall into greater decay whilst living at the Manor House with the Thompsons. The Palace was very dilapidated, only one wing remaining habitable. Anthony later became M.P. for Huntingdon from 1702—1705. In 1711 he was treasurer for the British Forces in Spain. He died in Fleet Prison in 1738 which was a debtors prison. He had two sons Thomas and James, the younger son becoming a well known poet. Thomas eventually inherited what remained of the Palace, but about the time that he was married in 1742 he decided to sell the Palace with the Manor and it was bought by Robert, Duke of Manchester.

Robert's son George inherited the Palace on his father's death in 1762, but he had little interest in the property and apparently had what remained of the Palace pulled down in 1789. All that remains of the Palace today are the abutments of a moat bridge (about 230 metres south of the Church).

THE CHURCH OF ST JOHN THE BAPTIST

Although the Parish Church is not quite in the centre of the village the top of the tower, capped with its small spire and weather vane, can be seen quite clearly as you approach Somersham along the St. Ives Road. Indeed you can pick it out amongst other buildings as you come down Pidley Road.

There is no mention of a church in Somersham in the Domesday Book of 1086, however, that does not mean that there was not one in the village. It is thought that there may have been one or more wooden church buildings from the 7th century onwards. There is, however, mention of a Rector of Somersham in 1221 and of a Vicar who witnessed a charter about 1225.

The present church is built of rubble with dressings of Barnack stone. The term rubble just means that the stones were of different shapes and sizes, often uncut, but does not mean that it is of poor quality. The stone quarried at Barnack, near Peterborough, was a valuable building material and was used for the quoins (corners), window openings and buttresses. Building is believed to have been started in the middle of the 13th century with the construction of the chancel. The smaller stones that can be seen from the outside at the top of the chancel seem to indicate that its roof was raised at some time.

The East Window of the Church

The tall, narrow pointed lancet windows in the chancel, three in the south wall, four in the north, with the east window made up of a group of three lancets, are characteristic of the Early English period. The east window is a memorial to the Somersham men who lost their lives in the 1914-18 War. The central figure is a representation of the Ascended Christ, with the new Christian warriors (St. George, St. Alban and St. Martin) on the one side, and the old Biblical warriors (King David, Gideon and Joshua) on the other, whilst the archangels Michael and Gabriel also figure in the design. At the foot the names of the fallen are inscribed on the panels. It was dedicated on 28th May 1922. Initially permission to install the window was given on condition that the men's names were not inscribed on the glass, but this objection was later withdrawn. There are two other stained glass windows in the lancets either side of the sanctuary. The one in the south wall is to the memory of Miss Bertha Eleanor Davies Mason. The other is in the north wall, and was put in by the Rev. F.D. Perrott, in memory of his mother and is dated 1883.

In the south wall of the sanctuary, between the altar rail and the East Window, there is a double piscina (a stone bowl and drain) one for the washing of hands and the other for cleaning the communion vessels and a sedilia (stone seats) at different levels, the highest being intended for the priest, the next for the deacon and lowest for the sub-deacon, both of these features are part of the original building. On the floor to the north of the altar is the one surviving brass in the Church. It shows a priest holding a chalice and wafer, it was renovated in 2012. Slightly further west on the south wall is the priest's door. The ornate brass candelabrum was presented to the church in 1787. The heavily carved oak chair was presented to the Church in 1912.

There is a sealed doorway high up in the north wall of the chancel just behind the fine pointed arch that separates the

The Piscina and Sedilia in the Sanctuary

chancel from the nave. This would have been the doorway to a rood loft.

Rood comes from the old English word meaning 'cross'. It would have been a carved cross bearing the body of Christ, flanked by the figures of the Blessed Virgin Mary and St John the Baptist. The rood loft was constructed in about 1485 from bequests from wills and would have stretched completely across the chancel. It is known that parts of some services were sung from these lofts, and it is thought that they preceded organ lofts with musical instruments being played from them. In Somersham Church you can see the entrance to a staircase in the south-east corner of the north aisle where singers and musicians would have accessed the loft. A rood loft would usually be supported by an open wooden rood screen and there may have been one in Somersham Church. During the Reformation in 1548 roods and their lofts were taken down by order of the Privy Council.

The nave was built about the same time as the chancel and is separated from the aisles by four pointed arches; the piers supporting the arches have moulded capitals finished with a small castellation.

In the late 14th century the roof of the nave was raised to make a clerestory – an upper storey of the nave walls pierced by windows above the roofs of the aisles. The word clerestory means clear storey and was important for allowing more natural light to enter the building, light being very important in Christian worship. The timber roof would have been constructed at this time, probably replacing a thatched roof which would have needed a much greater pitch to allow rain water to run off. There are some interesting carved bosses at the intersections of some of the roof timbers. Their purpose is to hide joints but they were used by wood carvers to show their skills and the bosses still have traces of paint on them indicating that they were almost certainly highly decorated. Also to be seen are a number of carved stone corbels that were designed to support the beams of the original roof. Outside the building on the eastern ridge of the nave stands a stone crucifix with the body of Christ on it. There was a similar crucifix on the eastern ridge of the chancel, but it was blown down in a storm in 1947 and lost its head and both arms. Some early photographs of the Church show crosses on both ridges. The remains of the damaged cross can be seen inside the Church.

The north aisle is used as a Lady Chapel and there is a single piscina in the wall to the left of the small altar. Two of the windows in the north aisle, the east window and the middle one east of the porch appear to have been changed and are of a 15th century style. At the western end of the aisle is a stained glass window depicting St George, the patron saint of England, dedicated to the memory of Richard Brown who died on 22nd November 1915.

The south aisle has a double piscina in the wall near its east end and in 1975 it was made into a memorial corner. It has a votive stand with candles and a memorial book in a glass topped wooden cabinet, the pages of which are turned regularly.

At one time the walls of the aisles were stenciled with designs which have been covered over with a thick coating of lime-wash. Some of the designs can still be seen on parts of the wall above the internal door to the north porch and either side of the west end arch, where the lime-wash has flaked off.

The north porch is believed to have been added about 100 years later than the north aisle and possesses some interesting features. In one corner there is a holy water stoup, a relic of the days when Roman Catholicism was the established belief of this country. It would be filled with holy water so that worshippers could make the sign of the Cross on their foreheads before they entered the church. Over the doorway to the nave is a niche for an image.

The south porch is thought to be a 15th century addition to the church. It is larger than the north porch but also has a niche over the nave doorway. On the outside can be seen the remains of a sundial. Also outside the south porch at the bottom of the tracery for the door arch are two stone carved heads. There are a number of similar carved heads at various points around the outside of the church. They are practically all in good condition, so much so that they may be replacements of original carvings as they show a lot of detail in the faces.

Apparently there was what Charles Dawes describes in his book as 'an ugly painted gallery, which disfigured the west end' of the church. It was erected to accommodate musicians and was removed during the curacy of Dr. Pinnock (1850 – 1871) to make room for an organ. The organ can be seen in one of the earliest pictures of the interior of the church. This was moved in 1855 when an organ chamber was built onto the south side of the chancel. The west end was thoroughly restored at this time as the arch had formerly been bricked up, probably when the gallery was erected.

The font was given by the Rev. Alfred Ollivant, D.D., who was Rector from 1842 to 1849. Close to the font lies a medieval chest which has been made from a single piece of wood that has been hollowed out. Originally it had five locks and probably could not be opened unless the five men who held the keys were present. It may have been where the written parish registers were once kept after it became compulsory to keep them in 1538.

The old wooden box pews

The earliest photographs of the inside of the church show wooden box pews on both sides of the nave and rows of three individual chairs in the centre of the nave. The choir stalls in the chancel were also smaller than the present ones. An old parish magazine explains how the churchwardens *"very fairly and impartially and according to the best of their powers, assigned sittings to the most regular worshippers at the Parish Church, and to those Parishioners who have applied for seats. Other worshippers are kindly requested to sit on the remaining "Free" Seats and Chairs, when the Church doors are opened"*. It continues *"All Parishioners are, at common law, entitled to accommodation in the Parish Church – that is to be seated – but not to a Pew"*. Presumably the "Free" seats were those in the centre of the nave.

In 1915 Miss Nix and Mr. Stanley Nix gave money for the re-flooring of the nave and to renew entirely the pews in memory of their brother Fleet Surgeon Nix RN. (a memorial plaque to him is on the wall of the south aisle). Then in 1927 when Mr. Stanley Nix died his widow gave further money for new oak choir stalls to be dedicated to his memory.

The tower was built early in the 14th century, later than the chancel and nave. It was built in three stages as can be seen from the varying sizes of the stones used in its construction. In 1552 there were four bells and a sanctus bell; in 1712 they were referred to as five very indifferent bells. Today there is a peal of six bells, which were all cast in 1782 by Edward Arnold of St. Neots, though the bell frame is much older. The bells were re-hung in 1902 and taken down and repaired in 1934. At some point in time a stairway up to the bell ringing chamber was built, it being accessed through a door near the west side of the north porch. In 1885 the clock and chimes were installed and dedicated, having been presented by Mr. W. J. Nicholls in memory of his wife.

Various repairs and improvements have taken place in the last 100 years in addition to those that I have already mentioned. The following are some of the most significant.

The present organ was installed in 1908, it was thoroughly cleaned and repaired in 1932 and an electric blower was installed, the organ having hand bellows up to that time. In 1976 the stone arch above the organ was found to be in a dangerous condition and the organ was not used until the repairs were completed. In 2005 the organ loft floor was replaced, the organ dismantled and cleaned and the great sound board, which had suffered water damage, was rebuilt.

In 1931 the chancel roof timbers were replaced and in 1970 the Church was closed for six months for urgent repairs to the roof after death-watch beetle was found. Further work was needed on the nave roof in 1979.

Base of the Tower before and after remodelling in 2013

Central heating radiators were installed in 1912 and a new gas boiler was fitted in 1961. In 1949 a scheme was approved to install electric lighting, prior to that there was gas lighting.

There are various monuments and plaques within the church the details of which are in the booklet 'A Brief History of the Parish Church of St John the Baptist, Somersham'. It also contains many other details of the church that I have not written about.

In 2008 the pews that were at the back of the church, behind the line of the font, were removed to create a social area with some tables and chairs. Plans were also submitted to the diocese to remodel the back of the church, in particular the area at the base of the tower which is used as a vestry. After several years of frustration caused by difficulties in getting the necessary approval and funding, work started in January 2013 and was completed in June of the same year.

The Benefice
A benefice, or living, in the Church of England describes any ecclesiastical parish or group of parishes under a paid minister. The Somersham Benefice covers the parishes of Somersham, Pidley, Oldhurst and Woodhurst, but that has not always been the case. Woodhurst was only added to the Somersham Benefice in 2010 and for much of the time up to the present century the benefice consisted of the parishes of Somersham, Pidley and Colne. The minister in the Somersham Benefice is called a rector.

You may wonder what the difference is between a rector and a vicar and even a curate. A rector is one type of parish priest. Historically they were supported by tithes, a form of local taxation of ten per cent levied on the personal and agricultural output of the parish. A vicar is a representative, deputy or substitute: anyone acting as an agent for a superior (probably a rector). A curate is a person who is invested with the care, or cure, of souls in a parish. So they are commonly used as assistant clergy.

Somersham has a particularly interesting history in respect of these three types of office. The earliest recorded Rector of Somersham was G. Grim in 1220 whose patron was the Bishop of Ely. Over the next few hundred years there was a succession of rectors, either under the patronage of the bishop or the king.

In 1605 when King James I decided to create a new professorship at Cambridge University, he funded the position by providing the professor with the income of Somersham Church. This Regius Professor of Divinity would then find a junior clerk to do the services for the community, pay him a pittance, and keep the rest of the cash. Over the next three hundred years it was the Curate who was the resident cleric and who lived in the Rectory with his family. Two junior curates looked after the parishes of Colne and Pidley.

This constitutional arrangement lasted until 1882. The passing of the Somersham Rectory Act of that year made the Bishop of Ely the patron and the living became a vicarage with up to two curates subordinate to the Vicar. However, half the income from the benefice still reverted to the University for another 50 years. This anachronism was not finally put right until 1934 with the passing of a further Somersham Rectory Act and the village had a resident rector.

In July 1934 the Rector wrote in the Parish Magazine *My Dear Parishioners. After more than fifty years "Rectory Lane" has come into its own once more. It leads as it used to do, to a Rectory and not a Vicarage. I am sure the old cottages are smiling with satisfaction under their thatched roofs.*

The Burial Ground Extension under construction in 2011

The Churchyard

The gravestones in the Churchyard date from at least 1736, and possibly earlier. However, years of weathering have erased the inscriptions on the oldest ones. The original Rectory (pre 1820) stood on a piece of ground that is now part of the Churchyard, probably somewhere near the Dovecote.

In October 2011 the burial ground was extended. Although it had been extended on several occasions in the past, this time it was remarkable for a number of reasons. Firstly it had taken over seven years to establish a right of entry for machinery to gain access to the site. Secondly because the ground was a few feet below the existing burial ground and a vast quantity of soil had to be imported onto the site and levelled. This took about five weeks to complete and about 18 months to settle. An interesting feature in this extension is the ancient 'Buck Well' which is now clearly visible as it has had a brick wall built around it.

The Parish Registers

The Church registers of baptisms, marriages and burials date from 1558 and, with the exception of those currently in use, are kept at the Huntingdonshire Archives where they can be inspected. It is curious that most of us have no idea as to when and why parish registers were started.

The registers were a by-product of the English Reformation, the break with the Roman Catholic Church and the adoption of Protestantism which began in the reign of Henry VIII. One of the immediate concerns of the king and his ministers was that the clergy fully understood that the king was the supreme head of the Church of England and that both clergy and the people were weaned away from Catholic practices. Accordingly a series of directives was produced by Parliament and the Crown, including the 'Injunctions to the Clergy 1538'. They contained instructions to, amongst other things:

- *provide a copy of the Bible in English in the parish church and exhort every person to read the same;*
- *teach parishioners by rote the Creed and the Ten Commandments and examine every parishioner at Lent;*
- *deliver one sermon every quarter based on the gospel of Christ;*
- *keep a register.*

The paragraph regarding parish registers included the following:

That you, and every parson, vicar, or curate within this diocese shall for every church keep one book or register, wherein he shall write the day and year of every wedding, christening, and burying made within your parish for your time, and so every man succeeding you likewise; and also there insert every person's name that shall be so wedded, christened, and buried; and for safe keeping of the same book the parish shall be bound to provide, of their common charges, one sure coffer with two locks and keys, whereof the one to remain with you and the other with the wardens of every such parish wherein the said book shall be laid up.

Despite the 1538 order many parishes did not start to keep registers until some years later. In 1598 it was ordered that registers should from then on be kept on parchment because the paper in the books that had been used since 1538 had been of poor quality and many entries were already illegible. The order stated that existing entries in registers were to be copied on to parchment, *especially* the entries for the period since Queen Elizabeth's accession in 1558. Unfortunately, some priests therefore decided to copy only those entries made since 1558 and that is probably the reason why the Somersham Parish Baptism and Marriage Registers start in 1558, although the Burial records only begin in 1563.

NON-CONFORMIST DENOMINATIONS

Baptists

It would appear that as early as the middle of the 17th century nonconformity had been established in Somersham. The records of the Baptist Church at Fenstanton show that at a meeting held on the 5th April 1653, Edmund Mayle declared their proceedings at Over, Bluntisham and Somersham. The Fenstanton Church registers record the names of members from 1645 to 1692 who went to Somersham and a number of other villages to see different Church members.

About 1770 Thomas Ladson, a zealous Baptist Minister of Needingworth, who frequently visited Somersham, preaching in houses opened for him, to the great annoyance of the church curate, was summoned to appear at the Huntingdon Assizes for holding a conventicle *(a secret or unauthorised assembly for worship)* and creating a disturbance; but the prosecution failed because Ladson was protected by the "Act of Toleration" which had recently come into force.

The curate's action appears to have strengthened Mr. Ladson's cause, for shortly afterwards a cottage at the bottom of Church Lane (now Church Street) was converted into a permanent Meeting House for his followers. A graveyard attached to this Meeting House is still in existence, being, probably, one of the smallest in Britain.

On the death of Mr. Ladson, the services seem to have been given up in his Meeting House, and most of his followers appear to have migrated to Bluntisham, to join the congregation of a good and zealous Baptist Minister, Rev. Coxe Feary. The following is a quotation from Coxe Feary's Journal *"May 17th, 1786. This evening I walked to Somersham, and for the "first time" preached there, from Ephesians ii. 1, 3. The barn was very full; my mind was in some degree at liberty; the people very serious, and I hope the Lord was with us of a truth."*

Coxe Feary's members and friends at Somersham, to whom he preached lectures, wanted a more comfortable place than the barn in which they worshipped for their occasional meetings. They purchased some ground and a "very neat Meeting House" was erected which was opened in the spring of 1812.

The Baptist Church of Somersham was formed on the 15th October 1818, with twelve members from the Baptist Church at Bluntisham and Joseph Belcher became the first pastor in March 1819.

In 1830 the Chapel was enlarged, and a new gallery added. In 1867 it was restored, re-pewed and supplied with a new organ. In 1874 Thomas Willson enlarged the vestry with money left him by Mr. J. Leake, to be spent at his own discretion for Chapel purposes. In 1876 Mr. Robert Childs generously purchased a 'neat dwelling-house' in the High Street, and presented it to the Chapel for a Minister's residence. The Chapel-yard contains a few gravestones to the memory of former members of the congregation.

In the early 1990s the Baptist Chapel was refurbished. Most of the pews downstairs were removed and replaced with chairs. The pulpit tends not to be used now, and it is hidden by a projection screen which is used to display the words of new songs, as the congregation uses a style of worship led by a variety of instruments, such as guitars.

Some members of the Baptist Church in period costume
celebrate the 200th Anniversary of the opening of their Chapel

On Saturday 19th May 2012 members of the Somersham Baptist Church celebrated the 200th anniversary of the opening of their chapel. Members processed in period costume from the Victory Hall to the chapel as a reminder of the faith of those who established the Baptist Church in the village. On the following day a commemorative service was held in the style of 1812 with the Rev. Bruce Daniels reading some of the first sermon preached by George Whitfield which saw the establishment of the church. He did have to edit a good hour out of the sermon!

Wesleyanism was introduced into Somersham in 1841 by Mr. Tollady and Dr. Leigh, M.D., of St. Ives. They re-opened Mr. Ladson's old chapel at the bottom of Church Lane for their services. The efforts of Tollady and Leigh appear to have been successful, for in four years they were able to build a Wesleyan Chapel in Squires Lane (now Parkhall Road), on land presented for the purpose by Squire Thompson.

During the 1990s the Chapel, which is brick built standing back a short distance from the road, was in urgent need of restoration. At an open meeting in 1997 it was agreed that there was a need for a Methodist presence in Somersham and that plans should be made to redevelop the building with the aim of making the premises available for use by the local community. Considerable financial help was available from the Central Methodist Church and the 14 members in the village, supported by other local Methodist Churches, set about fundraising. Unfortunately, in the meantime, the building continued to deteriorate and when insurance cover for public liability was withdrawn in 1999, it was necessary to close the Church. On the 19th September 1999 a Harvest Festival service was held in the chapel and it was sold to a private buyer in 2001.

Above the Wesleyan Methodist Chapel in Parkhall Road
Below: Chapel Members (late 19th century)

The Quakers settled at Earith about 1650. The ancient book containing the records of the Society of Friends there commences in 1655 with an account of the visit of James Parnell to the house of Francis Dun, at Colne. From an entry dated the 19th of August 1675, we learn that a meeting at Bluntisham was broken up by John Potts, of Somersham and Thomas Gilbie of Bluntisham, 'informers,' who reported to Nicholas Johnson, a Justice of the Peace, that it was a 'seditious conventicle'. He issued warrants to seize the goods and chattels of the Friends. The 'informers' were described as *"a company of loose, irreligious, profligate wretches, who were encouraged to plunder, rob, steal, break houses, commit burglary and make havoc and spoil their neighbours' goods, to serve the Church and King."* The victims of such harassment were frequently convicted in their absence, and often on false testimonies sworn by hidden informers.

One such victim was William Prior of Somersham, being a young man who having just finished an apprenticeship, was so poor that outwardly he had little or nothing but the clothes he was wearing. He was fined five shillings for attending a meeting. William was in bed when the officers of Somersham called and so they took away his clothes and left him with nothing to wear except one stocking, so he was forced to borrow clothes to cover his nakedness, until he had worked for more. His clothes were valued at ten shillings.

As far as is known there has never been a place of worship for Quakers in Somersham and most probably the Friends in the village attended the meeting house in Earith.

LOCAL CHARITIES

Historically there were a number of Local Charities. In 1876 Nathan Dews wrote about the Feoffees Estate, Perne's Gift, St Thomas's Money, Wilson's Charity and the Charity School. Over the years the scope and finances of these charities has changed. Today Somersham Parish Council retains an interest in a number of them; the Harvey Feoffees Charity, the Hammond Educational Foundation and the Somersham Charities of Poor's Money. The Parish Council only has responsibility for the William Petit Wilson, Robert Hempsted Charities of Poor's Money. The Harvey Feoffees Charity operates entirely separately; the Parish Council have representatives that sit on the board of Trustees. The Hammond Educational Foundation again operates in a similar fashion to the Feoffees and again the Parish Council have representatives on the board of Trustees.

The Feoffees is probably the most active charity.

On 18th May 1654 a Mr. William Harvey left an estate which was vested in feoffees (a group of trustees appointed to manage an endowed institution) upon trust, that the rents and profits should be applied for repairing and maintaining a bridge, called the Stone Bridge, at the east end of Somersham over a brook called Cranbrook, and leading from Somersham to Colne and that any surplus should be spent for repairs of the Churchway, leading from the bridge to Somersham Church, or some other public and charitable use within the parish.

The property consisted of the following:

Two tenements built on land allotted to the Feoffees, an allotment of one acre and two roods; also an allotment of two roods in Colne. An allotment of twelve acres in Somersham Fen and an allotment of seven acres and three roods on Somersham Heath.

The original Trustees were:

The Rector and Churchwardens of Somersham for the time being, and Rev. George Johnstone, Rector of Broughton and Messrs. Thomas Leeds, George Wilson, Charles J. Warner and William Mason.

The following is an outline of the many activities of the Feoffees since that time.

1771   The Trustees ordered a metal chest to be made for keeping and preserving the writing and belongings of the Feoffment, which was to be kept in Somersham Church.

An item appears in the accounts book, for the amount of twelve shillings and sixpence paid to Mrs. Bulleman for Liquor, purchased for the Feoffees meeting.

1792   Somersham's first street lamps were bought, 19 lamps were purchased.

1793   It was agreed at a meeting held in February, to have the lamps fixed in the street to be lit all night during the months of January and February.

1797   An order was made, that any person riding horseback on the pavement, with carts or wheelbarrows should be liable to a penalty of one shilling.

1839   27th May Trustees agreed to put a pump down near the Tithe Yard for the poor people of that area and in case of fire.

1844   17th April. Trustees received a plan from Mr. W.B.
        Prichard Engineers of Wilmington London for a new
        bridge to replace existing bridge called Pegspitt
        Bridge - cost £4. It was also agreed to put an advert
        in the Cambridge Chronicle and Cambridge
        Independent for tender to build.

        30th April accepted tender from Messrs. Headley Iron
        Founders of Cambridge for approximately one
        hundred and twenty pounds to construct the new
        bridge. Mr. Ibbott was instructed to demolish the old
        bridge for three pounds.

1854   It was agreed to lower the centre of the bridge six
        inches to effect better drainage from the Parish drains.

1864   A meeting was held on 11th April to agree that the
        Church Clock be removed above the bell tower
        window, and fitted with a new Copper dial, new
        minute working and new escarpment - cost not to
        exceed £30.

1874   It was resolved that the end of Church Walk near
        Tithe Barn be enclosed by gates. On the 7th
        September a sum of £15 was given to the
        Churchwardens for the purpose of erecting these
        gates.

1875   A sum of £40 was given to the fund being raised by
        the Trustees of The National and Charity School for
        the purpose of enlarging the school building.

1887   A contribution of £5 was given to the Churchwardens,
        towards the repair of the framework to the Church

bells. Also a contribution of £5 was given towards the repair of the Fire Engine.

1887   A subscription of £120 was given to the expense of lighting, the street light at the Cross to burn all night.

1894   A letter was received from the Parish Council demanding to see the funds and documents held by the Feoffees. It was decided to write to the Parish Council to point out that they had no authority under the law, and that the Council be informed in future communications that ordinary rules of courtesy be regarded.

The Feoffees House—33 High Street

1896   The Parish Council complained that the Feoffees did not keep a Minute Book and the affairs of the Trustees were very unsatisfactory. Feoffees replied,

56

that all meetings were recorded and enough had been said to make it clear, that the interference of the Parish Council was uncalled for.

1897   A new Feoffees House was constructed in the High Street and finished on 4th March 1898. This replaced the previous house that stood on the site.

1904   A ruling was made that the Clerk be responsible for all documents and not the village Clergyman. The Trustees decided to put a notice on the bridge, relieving them of all responsibility of any damage due to over laden vehicles.

1915   A letter was received from the Parish Council asking if the Feoffees would consider taking in hand the repairs and winding of the Church Clock. Feoffees agreed to accept payment of ordinary repairs and share the winding costs.

1938   The Feoffees were finding it difficult to finance the maintenance of the village paths, Huntingdonshire District Council were asked if they would take on this responsibility.

1950   Trustees discussed building a new bus shelter for the village.

1951   Bus Shelter now referred to in correspondence as 'Public Shelter'. Tenders had been received to build the Shelter of which W. Canham's tender was accepted for the sum of one hundred and seventy six pounds sixteen shillings and four pence. Final account for the Shelter was two hundred and thirty eight pounds thirteen shillings and eight pence.

1952   St. Ives R.D.C. enquired if the Trustees would consider selling off part of the Town garden allotments to facilitate the completion of Somersham Council houses.

1955   Somersham Women's Institute enquired if the Trustees would provide litter bins in the Village. It was agreed to provide one at the Cross and one at the Palace.

1958   The Trustees agreed to donate £100 towards the War Memorial. Sadly the Charity Commission informed the Trustees that this was not appropriate, as it was not a charitable purpose.

1964   Following a visit to Windsor Court by some of the Trustees, a television was obtained and presented for use in the general lounge.

1965   The Parish Council requested financial help to improve the street lighting in the village, to which the Trustees agreed to donate £200.

1968   A further request was made by the Parish Council for further improvements to the lighting. Trustees voted in favour of donating a further £200.

1973   More litter bins were purchased and fixed by the Charity in Parkhall Road.

1974   Miss Gale presented a Tithe map of Somersham Village to the Charity, to be kept with the Feoffee documents, with the condition it be made available for exhibition purposes within the Parish.

1976   It was proposed to move all important documents from the Church safe, to be kept at Huntingdon Record Office.

1977   The Somersham Feoffees, celebrated the Queen's Jubilee by purchasing and erecting a new flagpole on the Church. The Feoffees also purchased, and the Chairman Mr. Bernard Criswell presented, Crown pieces to all the children at Somersham School.

1978   The Parish Council accepted responsibility for the Public Shelter, as the Trustees could not afford to keep it in good repair, due to vandalism.

1979   Cambridgeshire County Council completed the modernisation of the original Stone Bridge, in which they had incorporated the Feoffees Plaque of 1894.

1980   A new Parish notice board had been funded by the Feoffees Charity and fixed on the wall of the Black Bull.

1981   Thieves stole the Village Pump at the end of Station Approach in 1978, the Feoffees now had a new replica pump made and fixed in the same position.

1982   The Rector stated that the Feoffees should no longer be governed by a decision made in 1915 concerning repairs to the Church Clock as a lot of costs had been shared by the Church and Parish Council since then. It was agreed that each and every repair should be considered on request. This was also agreed again in 1985.

1983   The Feoffees Charity sold the remainder of the Town Garden Allotments, to facilitate the building of houses in Windsor Gardens.

1984   The Parochial Church Council requested financial help in re-gilding the Church Clock face, the cost was £703.65 of which £700 was paid for by the Feoffees.

1988   After many years of sharing with the Parish Council, the cost of winding the Church Clock, the Parochial Church Council had decided to electrify this mechanism at a cost of £1625. The Trustees agreed to meet the full cost.

1996   The Baptist Chapel were carrying out a large restoration programme, which the Trustees helped financially as requested.

1997   Following the completion of the Victory Hall, the Trustees purchased the furniture for the Norwood Room.

1998   Huntingdonshire District Council demolished the Public Shelter built by the Feoffees. The plaque that was built into the shelter, listing all Trustees when it was built, is being kept by the Parish Council.

1999   The Trustees were asked if they would like to help in financing the replacement of kneelers within the

Church. It was agreed to finance those kneelers required for the altar rail.

2000   Somersham Church £5000 towards heating repairs.

2002   £365 for refurbishment of replica village pump.

2003   £164 for 2 new flags for the Church.

2006   £117 repairs to the Church clock and £2639 Church repairs.

2007   £148 to service Church mowers; £95 New Flag for Church; £500 donation to MAGPAS; £221 Church clock repairs.

2010   £750 donation to MAGPAS; £450 donation for a new church mower.

2011   £600 to Parish Council to replace the Coronation seat at the Bank.

2012   £500 Contribution for new shelving in the library; £125 grant to Somersham Church to repair the memorial brass in the sanctuary; £400 donation to the Victory Hall to upgrade heating in the upper room; £1000 to Somersham Church for a security system to protect the lead roof.

2013   £57.50 to Somersham Church for supplying flowers for the Queen's Diamond Jubilee

The representative Trustees are elected by the Parish Council, but they do not have to be a councillor, they have to be re-elected every four years. Co-optive Trustees are elected by Trustees in office, and have to be re-elected every five years. The Rector of the Village is automatically an Ex-Officio Trustee.

Somersham Charities of Poor's Money, William Pettit Wilson & Robert Hempstead

The Charity Commission approved a scheme by which these three old charities are administered jointly by a body of trustees. It is believed that these were first amalgamated in the 1960s and the trust deed updated in the 1970s.

The Charity known as the **Poor's Money** started when a sum of £20 was paid to the parish officers for the use of the poor coming from a rent charge of £1 a year from land which belonged to the late Bartholomew Ibbott. At one time money from this charity was used to distribute coal to five recipients.

The Charity of **Robert Hempstead** was initiated by his will of 6th July 1883 which directed his trustees to set apart a sum of money which would produce £10 per annum to be distributed in coal to the poor who needed it. Like the Poor's Money, at one time it was used to distributed coal to about forty recipients.

The Charity of **William Pettit Wilson** was founded by his will that was proved at Peterborough on the 5th September, 1867 and reads as follows:

"To invest in the purchase of Consolidated 3 per cent annuities in the joint names of the Incumbent and Churchwardens, for the time being, of the Parish of Somersham aforesaid, such a sum of money (out of such part of my personal estate as the law permits to be appropriated by will to Charitable purposes) as will produce the clear yearly sum of two pounds sterling, which sum of two pounds I hereby direct to be distributed annually, for ever, on St. Thomas' Day, by the Incumbent and Churchwardens for the time being of the said parish, among such poor widows and widowers resident within the said parish, and in such manner as the Incumbent and Churchwardens for the time being shall think proper."

In the late 19th century it was reported that money from the charity was used to give mutton to widows and widowers and a few large families all of whom were paupers.

Today the Trustees use the income of the Charities for the prevention or relief of poverty in Somersham by providing grants, items and services to individuals in need and charities or other organisations working to prevent or relieve poverty. The present trustees meet twice a year.

The Hammond Educational Foundation

In 1746 Thomas Hammond left, in his will, a sum of £200 for a school to be established for the education of the poor in the Parish of Somersham.

After a donation of land by The Church Commissioners in 1767 the school was built in Church Street in 1782. The Foundation was established to provide equipment to enable the poor to be educated at the school and in 1908 a trust document was sealed at The Board of Education. It established that the trustees were The Rector of Somersham (as an ex-officio trustee), two members of the Parish Church, three Parish Councillors, and two from Huntingdon County Council as it was the education authority.

In 1964 the present school in Parkhall Road was opened and the old school building was sold. The money was shared between the Foundation and the Church Commissioners for educational purposes in the Parish of Somersham and the Parish Church respectively.

The Foundation's money was invested in the Charities Ordinary Investment Fund (COIF) which is overseen by the Charities Commission and the income from that is the Foundation's current source of income. Today the Foundation is in existence to support the education of children.

VILLAGE FEATURES

There are many features which give Somersham its unique character. I have chosen a few which are prominent in the village today and some which have now disappeared.

Somersham Village Sign

In January 2000 a competition was launched to have a village sign to mark the Millennium. The winner was Hilary Barry whose design depicts the Church, the Bishop's Palace, a bridge, bulrushes and a tench to symbolise the lakes, fruit trees and the ancient charter.

A local woodcarver was commissioned to translate the design into a hand carved wooden sign which now stands outside Somersham Town football ground and the original design can be seen in the Victory Hall and the Information Centre (Library).

The Cross marks the centre of the village and it has changed a great deal over the years. At one time it was probably the site for the old weekly market and fairs. Now it has a modern bus shelter that was erected by the District Council in 1998.

The bus shelter also serves a useful purpose because on many Saturday mornings during the year local organisations, and some individuals, book the shelter to hold a stall to sell produce or other goods for fundraising purposes. On the 1st December each year it is surrounded by crowds of local people who have come to witness the switch on of the village's Christmas lights.

The previous bus shelter was much smaller and constructed of bricks with windows and unfortunately suffered a great deal of vandalism. However, it was rather amusing that several elderly gentlemen would on most days sit and talk in the shelter but they were seldom, if ever, seen to catch a bus.

The 'White Post' dated 1773 is a scheduled ancient monument which stands at the junction of the St.Ives and Pidley Roads. It is said that prior to the fire of 1824 it was placed on the 'Cross', where Church Street meets the High Street. When the burnt-down premises were rebuilt the street was made narrower and the post moved to its present position. The 'Cross' before that time may have formed the village green and have been the place where the weekly market was held.

Near the top of the post is a small hole that goes right through it and it is said that in the old days (probably when it was sited in the middle of the village) it was possible on looking through the hole to see Ely Cathedral. However, this would seem rather doubtful as the village of Sutton lies directly between Somersham and Ely 'as the crow flies' and as Sutton is over twenty metres above sea level it probably obscures the view of Ely Cathedral.

Somersham Windmills
There were once three mills in Somersham, all of them smock mills. They had sloping horizontally weatherboarded sides and were topped with a cap that rotated to bring the sails into the wind by means of a fantail. They were said to look like the smocks worn by farmhands in the past.

One of these mills was on land which is now part of Chapel Fields and little seems to be known about it. The second was

The North Fen Mill   *Holdich's Mill*

situated at Mill Farm at North Fen. It had six sides, four sails and a fantail and is thought to have been taken down about 1930.

The oldest mill was one which stood on the north side of Pidley Road. It had six sides, four sails but no fantail, the cap was turned manually with chains. It was known as Holdich's Mill having been operated by several generations of the Holdich family, the last being John Holdich. He remembered fetching corn by horse and cart to be milled and then delivering it for one shilling a sack. On a windy night he could grind sixty sacks of meal, *"and that was very good pay for those days"* he said proudly! He told the story of being wagered that if he could carry eighteen stones of wheat from the Rose and Crown to the mill, he could have the wheat. He then lifted the sack up on his back and set off. But, he said, it got heavier than 18 stones but he would not put it down, so he made use of every gate on the way, he got home and claimed his prize. Good wheat was milled for flour, and bran for wholemeal flour, but towards the latter end of the life of the mill, white flour was being bought from shops and not directly from the mill. Village folk were not so dependant upon crops or gleaning corn, so mostly animal feeds were milled.

The Weir

The 'Weir' at the side of Park Hall Road

Very few people can remember the 'weir' which was in Parkhall Road on the right hand side as you go out of the village, probably somewhere near the location of Norwood Road. It was really a large water trough that horses pulling wagons would pass through as they came from the farms on the fen into the village. Its purpose may have been for cleaning the feet of the horses and the wheels of the wagons that they pulled in order to stop lots of mud from the fields being brought on to the more affluent part of the village. I have also been told that it may have been to swell the wooden wagon wheels when they became very dry in order to stop their iron tyres from slipping off. Filling in the weir was discussed by the Parish Council in 1912 but it is not clear when this actually happened.

The 'Lock-up'

Old photographs of Church Street show a small building in the road just outside the Church gate. It was known as the 'lock-up', although it was actually a building which originally housed the fire engine, however, at the far end of it there was a section where people could be imprisoned for a brief period before being taken to Huntingdon.

The 'Lock-up in Church Street

In 1939 the fire engine was replaced by a trailer and two hand pumps. The Parish Council in 1942 discussed providing an ambulance for use in the parish which would be paid for by public subscription and possibly the Feoffees Charity. The ambulance was purchased in 1943 and housed in the 'lock-up'. In 1945 it was deemed that the building was unsuitable for the ambulance and a decision was taken that it should be disposed of and the building demolished. The 'lock-up' was then used for storage and eventually removed in 1950.

The Norwood Field

In 1938 the Parish Council talked about purchasing land for a playing field, but with the coming of the war they did not manage to pursue this aim until 1945. A field in Parkhall Road that was deemed to be suitable was bought the following year for £550 with the aid of a grant and a loan. In 1947 it was named the 'Norwood Field' the name apparently being a combination of the names 'Norman' and 'Woodroffe' who were prominent business men in the village.

The Victory Hall

Fundraising for a village hall to mark the Allies' victory started just after the end of the Second World War. However, it took Somersham more than forty years to complete the scheme. Initially progress was slow and it was not until the new housing developments in the village saw an influx of people who got involved in the project, that the Victory Hall fundraising campaign was rejuvenated.

The fundraising committee owned land in Church Street which was sold in about 1984/5 as a site for the provision of a new Medical Centre and Car Park. The new Doctors' Surgery and Health Centre were built beside the new village car park by the middle of 1986.

The money realised from the sale of the land made it possible to make an application to obtain grant aid from Huntingdon District Council. In March 1985 the Parish Council gave their full support and backing for the project and in September of that year a grant of £15,000 for the project was obtained from the Leisure and Amenities Committee of the local authority. The Parish Council pledged a substantial sum from existing funds with the Carnival Committee also pledging financial support of approximately £3,000. A donation of £100 was received from Somersham Town Cricket Club and there were further donations from other clubs and individuals in the village. Eventually it was possible to finance a project costing in total £61,600.

The Victory Hall in Parkhall Road

The building of the hall started during the winter of 1986/87 and was completed in 1991. On completion the hall came into regular use and was available for letting. The hall was officially opened on 17th December by the Rt. Hon. John Major who was the local MP and Prime Minister. He unveiled a plaque to mark the event.

The Victory Hall continues to be a popular facility in the village and is used on a regular basis by a number of local clubs and societies as well as being available for hire for private functions.

The Millennium Pavilion

In the 1990s the Parish Council decided that Somersham needed an additional playing field so that organised sports teams could be taken off the Norwood Field. In 1997 they secured a grant from the Sports Council for the full amount of £276,683 to develop such a field with a pavilion and car park. Work took several years to complete but at the end of May 2003, England and Warwickshire Cricketer, Nick Knight cut the ribbon to open the Millennium Sports Field. It has become the home ground for Somersham Town Cricket Club. It is also used by junior football teams and the large room in the pavilion is let to local clubs and societies as well as for private functions.

The Millenium Pavilion

The Lake

Most Somersham residents will need no introduction to the Lake, although those who have lived here for a good number of years also know it as the 'ballasthole'. The Lake was originally formed when it was used by the railway company as a ballast pit - hence the name. The 'bally-hole', its abbreviated name, was used for swimming in the summer and ice-skating when it was frozen over in the winter.

When the Windsor Green Estate was built, the Lake was

73

partially filled in, and then in 1975 it was purchased by Somersham Parish Council. A sub-committee, funded by and responsible to the Parish Council was set up, known as the Somersham Lake Committee. Its purpose was to improve and maintain the paths, hedges, banks, etc. Many young trees have been planted, and two islands created by floating materials across on a raft and sinking it.

Various species of birds use the Lake and island, including grebes, mallard, herons, terns, swans and Canada geese. As the vegetation becomes more established it is hoped that more will arrive.

Fishing is restricted to Somersham residents, guests may fish if accompanied by a resident. The stock of fish is low due to blue

Skating on the frozen waters of the Ballast Hole
The railway trucks can just be seen in the background

A view across the Lake

green algae, which has attacked the Lake several times. Plans are in hand to improve the quality of the water.

The Nature Reserve was officially launched in May 2010. It is a twenty three acre sight which includes the Lake, woodland and grassland. The area has been designated as a 'Local Nature Reserve' for its wildlife value, its value as a local amenity and also as an educational resource. Part of the site is also a 'Country Wildlife Site' because of the area of wild flower rich grass land. Much of the reserve follows the former railway line and appropriately has a level crossing gate at its entrance as well as a short length of the original railway track. Most of the work in clearing the site and maintaining it is carried out by regular working parties made up of volunteers.

In 2012 the Nature Reserve Group began work on establishing a Community Orchard in the north east corner of a part of the reserve that is designated as a dog-walking field. They were able to do this as they had secured funding. A substantial fence was erected with access gates to protect the area. Thirty fruit trees were planted on a special family planting day on 6th January the following year.

The entrance to the Nature Reserve from Station Approach

LISTED BUILDINGS

Listed buildings are ones that are acknowledged by the Secretary of State for the Environment to be of special architectural or historic interest. There are more than fifty listed buildings in Somersham, but the Parish Church of St John the Baptist is the only Grade I listed building. Grade I is only given to buildings of exceptional interest.

For those who live, work or otherwise have an interest in a listed building the main implications are:

- It needs to be maintained in reasonable order. The local council has reserve powers to intervene when necessary.
- Most internal and external alterations require listed building consent.
- Special consideration is given to the affect proposals requiring planning permission may have on the general setting of the listed building.

Owners of Listed Buildings are responsible for keeping them in good repair.

The Tithe Barn dates from about 1600 AD. It is a timber-framed, weather-boarded barn with a tiled roof.

Originally it would have been thatched and it had two long thatch fire hooks hung on the north wall facing the street. These would have been used to pull the thatch off the building in the event of fire. The barn would have been built to store the large quantities of grain that had been collected as tithes. In the 19th and 20th Centuries it was used for purposes such as flower shows, bazaars, children's festivals and other public entertainments then later used to house chickens before being converted into its present use as homes.

The Tithe Barn

Cranbrook Farm is said to be the oldest dwelling house in the village. It is a thatched timber framed building with some wattle and daub rendering, a brick gable end with a 19th century two-storey gault brick house-like addition at the other end.

Cranbrook Farm

It was originally built about 1492, so it is early Tudor with the classic layout for a Medieval Hall with an east and west wing, cellar and well at the back of the building. A fire would have burned in the middle of the building where the remains of bones and charcoal have been found. It was modernised in 1658. A floor and chimney were put in and papers (dated 1658) written by the owner Goodman Baird were found behind timbers that have been removed. The brick gable may have been built about 1806, a coin of that year being found under the corner post.

There are deeds which date back to 1750, which have been mislaid at present. On the 1838 Tithe Map of Somersham John SHEPPERSON is shown as the owner with William Harlott as the occupier.

1841 Census shows the following:

High Street	William HARLOT	60	Farmer	Yes
	Mary HARLOT	50		Yes
	Matthew HARLOT	30	Ag. Lab.	Yes

(Yes indicates that the person was born in Somersham)

Assuming that the neighbours in 1841 and 1851 were the same, the 1851 Census shows the following occupants:

High Street	William DARBY	59	Farmer (40 acres) B.Somersham employing 2 labourers
	Sarah DARBY	57	Wife	Thrapston
	William HODSON	16	Farm Servant	Somersham

In the absence of the deeds further occupancy becomes more uncertain.

The current owners bought the property in an auction in May 1985. They have been responsible for the renovation of the oldest parts of the building. This involved taking the building apart carefully and systematically, numbering the timbers in order to facilitate reconstruction. Many new timbers had to be cut and shaped to replace those which were no longer usable. Finally the roof had to be re-thatched. The top half of the medieval doorway and top half of the mullion window are original features. A simple canopy has been installed over the doorway using the original pin holes.

The Manor Hall is in Parkhall Road and has two 16th century end chimney stacks which were thought to be part of a former wooden framed building. A plaque on the building states that Squire Thompson rebuilt the house in about 1720. It is built from red brick and originally had three storeys with a parapet. There is a moulded brick band between the storeys. After a fire in the top storey, towards the end of the 19th century, the roof was redesigned to its present plain tiled roof with boarded eaves. The central front door with semi-circular metal work above it was the original front door to the house in the 18th century, when the two current front doors were windows.

The occupancy of the Manor Hall can be traced back to 1681 when Thomas Thompson lived there with his wife Phoebe (nee Hammond). Anthony Hammond and his mother stayed with them after the death of his father (also Anthony) in 1680. The index to the 1838 Tithe Map tells us that George Thompson was the owner and occupant at that time, he died in 1848.

The 1861 Census shows that Elizabeth Johnson was the head of household with 3 younger sisters. The house was being used as a school with 3 female pupils between the ages of 10 and 13. Two sisters are listed as governesses while the youngest Harriett is listed as having no occupation. The following Census reveals that Elizabeth had married Solomon Woodroffe, a Grazier with 30 Acres employing one labourer. Elizabeth and her two sisters are still running the school which now has 19 female and 4 male

The Manor Hall before the fire and as it is today

pupils aged from 3 to 16 yrs with one governess (teacher). There is also a housekeeper and 3 domestic servants one of whom is male. The household is very much the same in the 1881 Census except that the school now has 10 female pupils aged from 7 to 16 yrs with 3 governess's (teachers) one of whom is Elizabeth's younger sister Harriet.

There is no entry for the Manor Hall in the 1891 Census and by the 1901 Census the house had been substantially rebuilt after a fire, with the top story removed and it was divided into two as there are two entries in the Census. One side of the building number 21 was known as 'Homeleigh' and was occupied by Joshua Goodenough the village chemist who lived there from 1914 until 1931. After his death Joshua's spinster daughters Florrie, Constance & Ethel Goodenough, lived there until 1937.

The Old Rectory at the end of Rectory Lane was built in 1820 at a cost of £1,830. It was to replace a previous Rectory that stood on a plot of land which then became part of the churchyard. It is believed that the first occupant was John

Atkinson who was the curate at that time. The building was described in great detail in a document of 1822 as:

"One slated dwelling House in length 43 ft., in breadth 39 ft. within the Walls (i.e. internal dimensions), containing a dining Room, drawing Room, Parlour, Library, Pantry and Closet, under which are three Cellars. Over these are four lodging Rooms, with three dressing Rooms adjoining them. Attached to the House, a Kitchen, Scullery, Laundry and Pantry, in length 43 ft., in breadth 19 ft 6 ins. within the Walls. Over these are three lodging Rooms. In the Yard, a Coach-House, Stable with three stalls, and Coalhouse, in length 44 ft., in breadth 12 ft. 9 ins. Item, two Necessaries (i.e.privies), a Place for Ashes, and a pump. All these buildings are covered with Slate and were erected in the Year 1821 [sic] adjoining the Rectory House a Lawn, Garden, Orchard and Plantations, containing 2 acres 3 roods, enclosed by a quick hedge."

The building was sold in the 1990s as it was far too large for the Rector in current times and a new Rectory was built in Rectory Lane from the proceeds of the sale. The old Rectory was split into two dwellings.

Park House was built on the site of the Bishop's Palace in 1802. It was the residence of Litchfield and Betsey Moseley and their children. It is unclear if the house was the property of the Moseley family, but certainly the 1838 Tithe Map indicates that the Farm land was the property of a Samuel Farmer Esq.

Litchfield Moseley died on the 27th December 1821 aged 59 and was buried on the 3rd January. A memorial to him, which is made of black slate, can be seen on the floor of the chancel in the Parish Church.

The 1841 census shows the occupants of Park House as:

Betsey Moseley	75 years old	
Robert Tabram Moseley	50 years old	
Jeremiah Moseley	35 years old	
Elizabeth Warboys	40 years old	Servant
Sarah Salmon	35 years old	Servant
John Harvey	13 years old	Servant

Betsey died on the 29th March 1842 and a memorial to her can also be seen on the chancel floor in the Church. Robert Tabram Moseley inherited the house and the running of the farm. In the 1851 Census he is described as being a farmer of 800 acres employing 35 labourers and his brother Jeremiah is also described as a farmer. They still had the same three servants as in 1841.

Robert Tabram Moseley died on 29th December 1859 and the 1861 Census shows Jeremiah Moseley as the Head of household at Park Farm, being a farmer of 800 acres employing 34 men and 16 boys. He had a wife Sophia Matilda and two nieces, Betsey and Anne. Amongst other members of the household Elizabeth Warboys and Sarah Salmon were still employed as servants. In 1875 Jeremiah died aged 69 and it would seem that Park House fell into disrepair and the land was divided into small plots for renting. His widow Sophia continued to live in the village and in 1891 resided at Tollington House, next door to the George Hotel in the High Street.

About 1880 Jonas Smith purchased the property and offered it for rent. Park House, after being thoroughly restored in 1881, was called Somersham Park House and became the residence of Frederic Street.

In the Census its occupants are shown as:

Frederic Street	43 years old	Farmer of 816 acres employing 29 labourers and 9 boys
Mary Street	47 years old	Wife
Stanley Street	5 years old	Son
Sarah A Wright	22 years old	Domestic Servant
Emily J Cookle	18 years old	Domestic Servant

The 1891 Census shows that Frederic Street was still at Park House, now giving his occupation as a 'Farmer Auctioneer etc.' It is said that he was well known in farming circles and a founder of The Shire Horse Society in 1887. However, the 1901 Census shows that the house was now occupied by Jonas Smith, aged 46, his wife Amelia, their four sons, a daughter named Ciss, and a domestic servant. In 1912 Park House and farm came into the possession of Walter Smith, one of the sons of Jonas. In 1922 Sidney Smith, Walter's brother, bought the farm and ran it until his death in 1960.

It is said that during the Second World War the house was used as a safe house for Special Operations Executive operatives and the grounds used as training grounds for Westland Lysander aeroplanes as the fields were similar to those in France. In November 1944, Flt Lt George Turner flew a Lysander from Park House Somersham for the RAF Film Unit, which was making 'School for Danger' for the Central Office of Information. Later called 'Now it Can be Told', it was premiered in February 1947, and told something of the Special Duties Operations.

In 1945 it is understood that the Farm Manager, Bill Hodges and his wife Audrey, lived in the farm cottage and then moved into a wing of the house. In 1956 Brian & Helen Hodge apparently lived in part of the house until around 1964 when the farm bungalow was built. At one time the drawing room was said to be used for motorcycle repairs, with a leaking ceiling and somewhat rotten floorboards.

Park House before it was renovated

Walter Smith's daughter Joan Dimock inherited the land and the buildings when her father died and the house passed to her grandson Simon Stevens in 1996. That same year the land was granted Monumental Land Status.

A Demolition Order that had been placed on the house was lifted in 1984 after the intervention of the Georgian Society and in 2002 Richard & Janine Johnson purchased Somersham Park

House and restoration commenced early that year. They moved into the property on Christmas Eve the following year.

The Dovecote is a round building, located towards the North West end of the churchyard and is believed to be late 18th century. Apparently it is one of only three round dovecotes remaining in Cambridgeshire.

The word 'dovecote' was widely introduced in the 20th century: before that these buildings were called 'pigeon houses' or 'dove houses'. Pigeons were valued for their meat, eggs, feathers, down and dung and they cost very little to keep as they forage for their food and have a strong homing instinct. The birds mate for life and produce many offspring.

The Dovecote, for which the church has sole responsibility, had deteriorated over the years despite self-help maintenance carried out by volunteers from the church congregation. In 2005 the dovecote was thoroughly restored with the help of grants. Prior to that work it had been revealed that the roof was unsafe, only being held together by ivy in some places, and that many of the timbers were showing signs of rot and would need replacing. When work started it soon became evident that most of the plate (the timber ring supporting the roof timbers) would have to be replaced. The restoration work included clearing of the ivy from the building; removing and retaining the unbroken pantiles and roof fittings for reuse; replacement of rotten roof timbers, including the plate, while retaining as much of the original wood as possible; re-tiling the roof using the original pantiles, where possible, and using reclaimed tiles to replace those missing or broken; replacing the door, door frame and door lintel in keeping with the original design and materials and making good the plasterwork to the inside.

The other buildings with Grade II listed status include some which would not be thought of as buildings in the conventional sense. The most modern of these is the telephone kiosk that stands at the 'Cross'. Designed in 1935 by Sir Giles Gilbert and made of cast iron, it is not unique as thousands were produced for use throughout the British Isles and in some cases beyond. Five of the milestones that are situated within the parish boundaries have Grade II listing. Three of them stand at the side of St. Ives Road and the other two at the side of Chatteris Road, being 3, 4, 5, 6 and 7 miles from St. Ives (and 28, 27, 26, 25 and, 24 miles respectively from Wisbech).

Whilst many other buildings in the village are Grade II listed, in my opinion the ones mentioned above are among the most interesting. Some of the others such as the Baptist Chapel, the Wesleyan Chapel and the Old School building (No. 5 Church Street) are mentioned in other parts of this book. I do not intend to belittle the other listed buildings, some of which are quite imposing and interesting to look at, particularly 'The Limes' and 'Mulberry House' (formerly 'The Chestnuts') which are of a similar design and construction; Wisteria House which has the monkey puzzle tree in the front garden; Braunston House at the Cross and 100 High Street both of which have undergone some renovation in recent years. However their details, and those of all of the other listed buildings in the village can be found by doing a search for 'Somersham' on the website www.britishlistedbuildings.co.uk/england/cambridgeshire/somersham.

ROADS AND ROAD NAMES

The names given to roads have always fascinated me. Many are obvious because of where they lead (e.g. Chatteris Road, Colne Road, Pidley Road and St. Ives Road), some because of a building (e.g. Church Street, Rectory Lane and Station Approach), whilst others have origins relating to former landmarks and local people. Modern roads are usually confirmed by the District Council from names submitted to them by Somersham Parish Council. Unfortunately the minutes of those council meetings do not record the reasons for the names, but one can speculate on what they might have been.

In my introduction I wrote that the village originally consisted for many years principally of one road about three quarters of a mile long running east west crossed by a second road near the centre. This is a simplification as there are other places and roads shown on the 1838 Tithe Map, although none in the centre are named, those out of the village (Pidley Road, Park Hall Road, Short Drove etc.) are named. Note that the road that today has the sign Parkhall Road was Park Hall on that old map. There is still some debate about whether Park and Hall should be joined into one word as it appears on the present day road signs and maps. There is a Park Hall marked on present day large scale OS maps, just past Short Drove, which would suggest that it gave its name to the road that leads to it.

An interesting name that appears in the index to the 1838 map is Butt Close. It is assigned to a plot of land where Butts Close is today. A Butt was formerly a shooting target, a mound for archery practice. Edward IV (1461 – 83) made shooting practice compulsory on Sundays and feast days. Every man between the ages of 16 and 60 was expected to own a bow of his own height, and every township was ordered to set up its own butts. Games that might prove counter attractions, such as football, were designated 'unlawful sports'. The longbow ceased to be an important weapon during the reign of Elizabeth I, so we can assume that the land marked on the 1838 Tithe Map as Butt Close was the site where Somersham men carried out their archery practice.

The 1887 Ordnance Survey Map does show some names: High Street, The Cross, Church Lane, Rectory Lane, King Street, Chapel Field Lane and Squires Lane. Church Lane is called Church Street today, having had its name changed sometime during the administration of St. Ives RDC. Squires Lane is the name given to the part of Parkhall Road from The Cross presumably just up to the Manor House where the Squire (Lord of the Manor) lived, a name that was dropped some time in the 20th century. Shepherds Terrace almost certainly has nothing to do with sheep, but is a name derived from an association which relates to the Loyal Lodge of Ancient Shepherds, who helped the poor of the parish. Pinfold Lane is shown, but not named although the houses are marked on the map. A pinfold was a pound in which stray animals were kept.

The only new road that appears on the 1920s OS map is that of Bank Avenue which may only have been recently built and is opposite to the bank of the Cranbrook. Most of the houses already existed along the bank and were known as Bank Houses. Incidentally in 1973, St. Ives RDC approved a recommendation from Somersham Parish Council that the area between the two entrances to Colnefields be renamed 'The Bank' and the properties renumbered. The reason for this was that in this section of the Chatteris Road, that had formerly been known as 'Bank Houses', there had been several new houses built between the existing properties so that numbering them sequentially was no longer possible.

Coronation Avenue was built before the war and Norwood Road was built in 1947. It would appear that the necessary land was purchased by St. Ives RDC in 1936, but the war disrupted the building programme. Coronation Avenue almost certainly got its name from the Coronation of King George VI. Norwood Road was originally called Parkhall Estate. Feoffees Road was probably next to be built. An old map shows that it was originally much shorter and did not link up with Norwood Road as it does now.

A postcard showing Norwood Road as Parkhall Estate

In the early part of the 1960s Queens Road, Bishops Road, Manor Close and Squires Close were developed. Their names all seem to be associated with the ownership of Somersham around the 17th century.

In the 1970s the population of the village almost doubled owing to the building of two housing estates. The Trundle which winds through one of them probably takes its name from Trundle

Wood, which is shown north of the Pidley Road on very old county maps. Two of the roads that branch off it are named after William Harvey (Harvey Drive) and Bartholomew Ibbott (Ibbott Crescent) who were both associated with local charities. I have no idea who the Robert (Robert Avenue) might be, but the way to the Lake (Lakeway), a ditch along fields (Ditchfields) seem almost self explanatory whilst a loftstead was an old type of landholding (Loftsteads).

The Grange Road estate, which was developed in the later part of the 1970s, takes its name from 'The Grange' (which is No. 65 in the High Street) and is built on some of its former farm land. Hereward Close derives its name from a house and farm 'Hereward House' that is No. 76 High Street. Six Bells was probably named after the public house that was in the High Street but this in turn probably took its name from the number of bells in the church tower.

King Street before modern houses were built on it

Although King Street had existed for many years it only had a few houses which were close to the High Street. It was developed further with new houses in 1986 and Whitehall Close, that is a spur off the street, must take its name from 'White Hall' home of Whitehall School.

The small estate that is almost at the end of Church Street has the names of three men associated with the setting up of the charity school. Thomas Hammond (Hammond Way) whose legacy financed the building of the school, the Rev. Daniel Whiston (Whiston Place) who played a vital part in making sure that Hammond's wishes were fulfilled and John Crane (Crane Close) the first schoolmaster.

Other late 20th century housing developments are Meridian Close which obviously takes it name from the Greenwich Meridian Line that runs through Somersham; and 'The Pastures' which is a shortening of 'Shepherds Pasture', the developer's preferred name 'Old Rectory View' was rejected by the Parish

'The Pastures' being built

93

Council.

AGRICULTURE

Somersham's location means that farming has always been diverse. To the north there are the flat fertile fens, once boggy, now drained and especially good for growing root crops. To the west is higher clay land. The soil is hard in the summer, wet and sticky all winter and with the advantage of modern machinery, it is good for growing cereals. The south is traditional fruit growing land and with Colne and Bluntisham, was once covered with plum, apple and pear orchards but few remain today. The land to the east was always more prone to flooding and some areas were only suitable for grass. Most winters people would skate on the frozen, flooded grassland beyond the Cranbrook.

Farming was very different in the past from what it is like today with the surrounding fields providing work for most of the men in the village. Horse drawn implements did most of the cultivation and horses pulled the carts that provided all local transport.

A writer in 1793 said that in Huntingdonshire

"the price of labour is 12d and 14d a day to common labourers, from the end of harvest until hay time begins; then 18d a day until harvest; and 2s 6d in harvest, with beer in times of carrying; and if hired by the month or for the whole harvest, about two guineas board and beer;—women 6d per day weeding; 10d hay-making; 1s harvest work. They work from light to dark in winter; and from six to six in the spring and summer months (except harvest, when they work from light to dark). The poor in general have dwellings suited to their station; as almost every one of them

may grow his own potatoes, and have constant employment if he pleases, they are naturally as little disposed to emigrate from Huntingdonshire as from other counties."

In 1813 a report was drawn up for the Board of Agriculture entitled '*A General View of Agriculture in the County of Huntingdon*'. In that report it stated that *"the parish of Somersham contained 2,100 acres of arable land, 369 of meadows, 300 of pasture, 16 of plantations and 15 of woods. The soil was described as consisting of 1,000 acres of clay, 200 of gravel and 1,400 of fen. The village was 'supplied by very good springs'. The owners of the estates were the Bishop of Llandaff, and Messrs. Farmer, Ansell, Ibbott, Leeds, Ilett and George Thompson. There were 40 farm houses, 80 dwelling houses and 120 cottages. The size of the farms varied from 50 to 500 or 600 acres. The tillage was by three horses abreast, fallow being ploughed three times. The cattle of Somersham were chiefly shorthorns; there were 87 cows, 119 stores; and 40 calves were reared. There were 148 horses, and 29 foals in the village. The 1,000 sheep consisted of the Lincoln and Leicester breeds. Labourer's wages were 12 shillings per week in winter and 15 shillings in summer, 17 shillings per week with meat and drink at harvest time."*

Fruit growing was an important part of the agricultural scene around Somersham and some of the neighbouring villages for many years. The Board of Agriculture's 1813 report describes how in 1806 *"William Margetts planted, on his estate in the parish of Somersham, an orchard of sixteen acres of land, with all sorts of the choicest fruit trees, apples, pears, plums and cherries. In a close adjoining Mr. Margetts' orchard, in the same year (1806) the Rev. John*

Somersham Fruit Pickers

Ingle planted an orchard of eighteen acres of all sorts of the choicest fruit trees, the trees are very healthy and promising." The closure of the railway in the 1960s was probably the first big setback for fruit growing in this area. It had provided a lifeline of rapid transportation and without it the number of suitable outlets for fruit became limited, added to this a gradual influx of cheap imported fruit in the later part of the 20th century finally made fruit growing unprofitable. This led to many orchards being left untended and others ripped up as the Government of the day recognised that maintaining unproductive orchards was not desirable and the demand for arable crops was increasing. Grants were therefore offered to help with the cost of tree removal.

The introduction of the railway in 1848 with the branch line to Ramsey opening in 1889 undoubtedly made a significant difference to farming as produce could be transported to distant markets. It was loaded onto wagons by hand at Somersham railway siding. Sparks flying from the steam trains would occasionally start fires in the fields near the line. If the horse drawn fire tender was called to deal with such an incident on fenland off the Chatteris Road, anticipating that it could take some time, the crew would call at The Wagon and Horses pub for a barrel of beer on the way!

Cattle often grazed beside the road as there was little traffic. Tending them was one of the first jobs given to boys leaving school aged 14. Sheep and cattle were driven on foot all of the way to St. Ives Market on a Monday. Reg Saint a farmer from along the Bank would drive his flocks of sheep through Somersham. If farmers bought livestock at St. Ives market they would walk it back to the village. Many fields were needed to grow grass for animal grazing and make hay for the horses. William Criswell used horses until 1959 and was one of the last farmers in the area to do so. There were two blacksmiths in the village, John Rilett whose forge was near the Baptist Chapel and Ralph Brooker whose forge was knocked down after the Second World War to provide the access for Feoffees Road to be built.

In the middle of the 19th century the first self-propelled steam engines for agricultural use were developed. There were three, possibly four, businesses operating heavy steam locomotives in the village which were available for contract work such as threshing, ploughing and cultivating. However, most farms were small and could not afford such equipment and they continued to use draught horses throughout the year, but during the harvest the contractors would travel from farm to farm hauling the threshing machine which would be set up in the field and powered from their traction engine. The threshing tackle would beat and separate the grain from the straw. One such business was run by the Kimpton family who operated traction engines from their yard in Parkhall Road.

Kimpton's (Haulage Contractor) traction engine

During the First World War the Board of Agriculture organised the Land Army, starting activities in 1915. As Britain was struggling for labour with three million men away fighting, the government wanted women to get more involved in the production of food and do their part to support the war effort. In 1939 as the prospect of war again became increasingly likely, the government wanted to increase the amount of food grown within Britain. In order to grow more food, more help was needed on the farms and so the government started the Women's Land Army.

Tractors were taking over a lot of the farm work by the 1950s, so there was less need for hay and with tractors making ploughing easier, even more land was brought into food production. In the 1960s chemicals were introduced to control weeds and harmful pests and diseases and this continued the downward trend in employment on the land. The world population was growing and marketing became more global, so in the 1970s and 1980s farmers were encouraged to increase food production. Machinery became bigger as did the size of the fields with the removal of hedgerows.

Farmers have always adapted to the demands of the time and now produce food more efficiently and with greater regard for the environment. Trees are being planted and field margins left to protect wildlife. Biodiversity is the new priority for modern farmers and they are the guardians of our countryside.

Allotments have been in existence for hundreds of years to give 'the labouring poor the provision of food growing'. Somersham is fortunate in having allotments on Chapel Field and behind King Street covering 42 acres.

The Feoffees Charity established a large number of allotments in 1844 on land that it owned. Some were on fenland, others on heathland, and the rest was garden land, the rents varying for the type of land, fen being the dearest. There were 94 tenants initially and they had to agree to the Feoffees rules which included that 'no tenant shall work his allotment on Sundays; or during the hours of daily labour, without the consent of his employer'. Also that 'all occupiers with their families will be expected to attend a place of worship on Sunday'. They were required to sign the agreement but only nine could write their names, the rest just making their mark. The vast amount of the land was sold over a period of time and now the Feoffees only have a small area of allotments which are situated along the Colne Road.

At the end of the First World War allotments became particularly important to maximise food production. Land was made available principally to assist returning servicemen (Land Settlement Facilities Act 1919).

In 1921, The Somersham and District Smallholding and Allotments Association was formed. The plots were a nominal 'forty pole' or 'rood' in extent (quarter of an acre) and every member or plot holder was expected to pay a minimum of 15 shillings which was one twentieth of the value of shares on that plot. The nominal value of a plot being £15. The money was needed to pay for the society to have a clerk.

Demand for, and cultivation of allotments has varied over the years. In times of recession people turn back to the land to produce food that costs less. The 'Dig for Victory' campaign in the Second World War also saw gardens and playing fields

An Advert used in the heyday of local fruit growing

101

turned into allotments. Gradually interest in growing fruit and vegetables on allotments went into decline but there has been a renaissance in recent years possibly spurred on by the desire to grow food organically.

PUBLIC UTILITIES

Today, in the 21st century, we take for granted things like the supply of electricity, gas and water, street lighting and sewage disposal. However, there was a time when none of them were part of everyday life.

Street Lights, Gas and Electricity

The first street lights in Somersham were installed in 1792 when the Feoffees Charity bought nineteen lamps which would have burned oil. The following year the minutes of the Feoffees state 'that the lamps now fixed in the streets of this parish are to be lighted up during the dark nights of January and February'. A further minute in January 1804 stated 'that the lamp at the Cross to be lighted for the winter season on dark nights'.

A very old street light at the Cross

In 1868 a gas works was built not far from Somersham Station. It was financed by the gas company which was formed on 11th

October that year with capital of £1425 made up of 245 shares of £5 each and a loan of £200. Coal gas was generated for Somersham and other local villages. The 'Gas House' that was adjacent to the gasworks still stands today and was renovated for habitation in 2012.

In 1869 the Feoffees paid a subscription of £12 towards gas lighting for the street lamps. They continued to do this annually provided that the remainder of the cost was covered by public subscription. In 1887 the cost had risen to £20 and from that year it was decided that the lamp at the Cross should burn all night.

Right up to the time of the blackout in the Second World War the streets in Somersham were only lit by gas lights. The gas lighters would come round on a cycle, with a long pole and taper and light the lamps in the streets when it was getting dark, and come and put the lights out again in the morning.

Electricity came to the village in 1935 but those people who can remember its introduction say that it wasn't very reliable at first. Electric street lighting did not come to the village until after the Second World War. The Hunts Post dated 10th October 1946 reported that when the Feoffees Chairman performed the switch-on, 52 lamps flooded the village with light from end to end. It was the first public street lighting that the electrical company had completed since 1939. However, some outlying areas of the village, including houses on the St. Ives Road, did not get electricity and street lighting until several years later.

When the Feoffees were approached by the Parish Council in 1964 who requested financial help to improve the street lighting in the village, the Trustees agreed to donate £200. Four years later another request was made by the Parish Council for further improvements to the lighting. Trustees voted in favour of donating another £200.

Water and Sewage

At one time many people had a well and a pump in their back yard. If not, they had to rely on public pumps that were in the street. There were five or six pumps in the village: two along the Bank, one by the doctor's residence (now Brookfield House) by Station Approach, one at the Cross where there was a pump on the wall, another by the Assembly Rooms in West End. By the avenue further down West End along the St. Ives Road, there was a double decker pump - it had two spouts on it. If a workman came in with a cart and a barrel on it, the bottom spout was blocked off so that the water could be pumped straight from the upper spout into the barrel on the cart. The water was considered to be very good and clear because the gravel in the soil acted as a filter.

A piped water supply reached the village in 1934 when Somersham was on the route of a new water main being laid to serve Ramsey and all properties on the way. As soon as the new water supply was available, the water from all the pumps was, overnight, declared unfit for drinking.

In 1953 mains sewage disposal came to Somersham. The relatively high water table and, in some places, the great depth of the work, made it a slow and tedious operation causing widespread disruption and annoyance over a long period.

Prior to that sewage was collected one night each week from every house by the two men with the 'night soil cart'. They would go to the privy in the back garden and take the bucket from under the lavatory seat and empty it into big buckets on the cart. The sewage stank when it was collected, which is why it was done at night. The men would take it to a place along Parkhall Road just before the bridge. They used to tip the sewage into a pit and when it was full they used to dig another one.

The Post Office and Telephones

Harry Clements is reputed to be the first person in the village to have a telephone in the early 1920s. He and his family lived at 57 High Street (known to older residents as the old post office). A small manual exchange was installed in the house which served twelve lines. The exchange was manned by his wife and sometimes his young son Dick, when Harry was out. However, the exchange was not very busy as for much of the time there were only five telephones in Somersham.

After the Second World War an automatic exchange was set up at West End Avenue close to the first council house in that road. Today the telephone exchange is situated at the end of Station Approach close to the entrance of the Nature Reserve.

Harry Clements was not only the telephone operator but I am told that he was also the postmaster. He used to travel to the main postal sorting office in Huntingdon and collect the mail for Somersham and all of the other local villages and would drop it off to each village post office. He also used his truck, which was a Model T Ford with an extended chassis, to carry out other haulage work.

Prior to Harry Clements the trade directories record Horace Whitworth (1903), Walter Littlewood (1906) Walter Webb (1910—1936) as being sub-postmaster and running the Post Office. They all appear to have been operating from the premises in the High Street next to the Rose and Crown Public House.

After Harry Clements the Post Office moved to the house next to the Baptist Chapel and was run by Mrs. Rollings. The wall of the house has a section of newer bricks where the post box used to be situated. The Post Office later returned to the general store next to the Rose and Crown. It still operates from the same shop which is now the One-Stop Shop.

The Old Post Office (57 High Street)

THE RAILWAY

Somersham Station was of great importance to the village for over one hundred years. The first significant event that occurred was on March 1st, 1848 when the "Wisbech and St. Ives Junction Railway" was opened for passenger traffic. This line was worked by the Great Northern and Great Eastern Joint Committee. It ran from St. Ives to March, with intermediate stations at Somersham, Chatteris and Wimblington, and had opened for freight a month earlier.

In March 1848 a local newspaper reported that:

"On Wednesday last, the 1st, the railway from St. Ives to Wisbech was opened with an excursion from Huntingdon, of which many persons availed themselves. About 700 persons left St. Ives, and on arriving at Somersham they were much pleased and interested. The station was crowded with the inhabitants, all of whom appeared to admire the sight so novel to them. A band

The Railway Line through Somersham Station

played, flags were unfurled, and upon the whole the scene was really imposing".

The next momentous occasion came on 16th September, 1889 when Somersham became a junction as the line from Ramsey East to Somersham opened. The Hunts County Guardian proudly announced the following:

"Monday last should mark an epoch in the history of the Huntingdonshire Fen district, as it witnessed the successful inauguration of the new Railway which connects Ramsey and Warboys with Somersham and St. Ives, and thence with the three great railway systems of the neighbourhood. As is well-known, the line, which is seven and a half miles long, has been constructed for over a year, during which time there have been various rumours, as to the date of opening, and much disappointment was repeatedly caused. We were enabled last week to authoritatively announce that at last a decision had been actually come to, and it was with much pleasure that we this week recalled that the long deferred inauguration is now an accomplished fact."

Some 25 years earlier there had been a scheme for a railway to connect Somersham with Holme. The promoters starting constructing the railway from Ramsey to Holme (then worked by the Great Northern Company), intending as soon as the necessary arrangements could be made, to carry it on to Somersham. At that time, however, the Great Eastern Company were promoting their "coal line" from the North direct to London, and their system came right through the route of the Ramsey promoters. So the G. E. Company bought from the Ramsey shareholders their line to Holme, at the same time undertaking to carry it on to Somersham as originally intended. After they had purchased this piece of line, for some reason or other, they did not carry out their decision as far as the

Somersham line was concerned, and applied to Parliament to release them from their obligation to make the extra piece of line. Although there was some opposition, the Committee of the House of Commons which looked into the matter, agreed to this request. Over the next thirteen years there was a lot of wrangling between the G.E.R. and the G.N.R. Companies and eventually a local syndicate, the Ramsey and Somersham Junction Railway Company, proceeded to build the line without assistance from the G.E.R. Company.

The quantity of land taken by the line amounted to eighty six acres, and the negotiations for the purchase were successfully carried out by the company's solicitor. It ran through lands of Lord de Ramsey, the Duke of Manchester and several other landowners as well as through the parishes of Ramsey, Bury, Wistow, Warboys, and Pidley-cum-Fenton. Many of the landowners, doubtless recognising the boon that the line would be to the district, treated the company very handsomely, and much of the land was transferred to them at purely agricultural value. In some instances, however, the promoters had to pay very heavily, notably for some land which cost them £240 per acre, the average price being about £40 per acre. Altogether the sum of £13,059 was spent on the purchase of the land.

During the course of construction there were very few difficulties. There were some heavy cuttings to make at Warboys, but these were carried out without much of a problem. What proved to be a valuable find and which represented a saving of about £1,200 to the Company, was made close to Somersham. A good seam of gravel was discovered beneath the land of Mr. George Wilson, which gave the contractors sufficient ballast for the whole line. The line was single track and there were three bridges and two stations, Ramsey and Warboys (Puttock Drove) and a siding at Pidley. All the station buildings

Somersham Station shortly before the line closed

were substantially built by the time the line was opened and those at Ramsey were regarded as picturesque, as well as comparatively spacious.   The second station at Puttock Drove was named 'Warboys', although it was a mile from the village. It was a very important one, as it took in the traffic from Wistow, Warboys Fen, and part of Ramsey Hollow.   Pidley was only a goods siding and took in the district of Pidley-cum-Fenton, Colne and Somersham Fens.

The district through which the new railway passed was immensely important.   In the vicinity of the line were 40,000 or 50,000 acres of the finest root growing and corn growing land to be found in the fen district, but because of the soft roads and difficulties of carriage of the crops, it had not received the development of which it was capable.   It had in fact only been waiting to be penetrated by a railway to leap into importance as one of the best root growing centres in the whole of the fens. As an effect of what a local line could do in an agricultural area you only had to look at Ramsey St. Mary's. Here the fenland was in many respects similar to that on the other side of the town, only that Pidley and the fens surrounding, was reputed to be far richer. Six months after the Ramsey and Holme line through St Mary's was opened, the land literally doubled in value and where a root was scarcely grown before, then there was little else to be seen. It was therefore reasonable to anticipate when the new line opened that there would be a similar development. The railway also made the market of St. Ives easier for the farmers of the district to access.

The local press reported in September 1889 that:

"The first train was timed to leave Ramsey at 8.10 am, and by that time the station was crowded by expectant passengers and lookers on. No less than 84 full tickets were issued and with the passengers taken up at Warboys and the railway officials, over 200 reached the junction at Somersham. At various points along the line of the route there were small crowds of people waiting to see the novelty of a train passing through the fens, and when Warboys was reached it was found that several of the oldest of the villagers were seated on chairs on the platform, having been brought from the village a mile away, in conveyances lent by farmers in order that they might witness the arrival and departure of the first train that ever passed through Warboys parish. It was remarked that some of the oldest present had never ridden in a train in their lives. The proceedings of the day passed off without a hitch."

When the train service first started many people used it, but passenger numbers naturally fell away as the numbers and speed of road vehicles increased. Only a few people travelled by each train with the exceptions of special occasions such as Warboys Feast and Bank Holidays, when as many as 60 had used the railway. At one time it was again suggested that the railway company intended connecting the Ramsey and Somersham line with the Ramsey and Holme line, but the idea was dropped, if indeed it ever existed. In September 1930 the railway company announced that the passenger train service on the branch line from Ramsey (East) to Somersham would be ended. The company's action was due to the fact that the passenger traffic on this line did not pay, and probably had not paid for some years. The last train referred to by locals as the 'Warboys and Somersham Express' ran on Saturday 20th September and no more was Somersham station to ring with the cry of "Change for Warboys and Ramsey!"

Goods traffic continued and was entirely unaffected because it paid for itself over and over again. Stock and agricultural

The Signal Box

produce were conveyed from Ramsey all over the country by rail, a large quantity being taken to and from St. Ives on market days. Eventually in 1956 goods services were withdrawn between Warboys and Ramsey East and in 1964 they were withdrawn between Somersham and Warboys. Two years later in April 1966 goods services were withdrawn from the St. Ives to March line and in March the next year there was complete closure of the line and much of the track was removed.

The Station

Somersham Station reconstructed at Fawley

The railway station at Somersham was erected about the year 1848, but many alterations took place after that date. New waiting-rooms and offices were erected on the down side, and a covered way provided on the up platform, which was later extended to take longer trains. The two platforms were connected by a footbridge at the south end of the station, next to the level crossing. There was no separate branch-line platform at Somersham, so Ramsey trains worked into and out of the main-line platforms in between other service trains.

When the railway was closed some of the station buildings, such as the handsome signal box, were soon demolished, and vandals left their mark on the platform accommodation, actually setting fire to one of the wooden waiting rooms. The fire brigade managed to contain the blaze. However in 1977 the station buildings were bought and dismantled by Sir William McAlpine who had them re-constructed and restored at his home at Fawley, near Henley-on-Thames where they still remain.

There have been a number of organised trips taking people from Somersham to Fawley to see the station. One in May 2009 saw two coach loads of villagers from Somersham travel to Fawley. They were greeted by Sir William McAlpine and had a very

The last passenger train on the line from Ramsey

enjoyable time looking around the station, riding in an open truck pulled by a small steam engine on the short length of track and looking at the memorabilia connected with the station and railways in general.

Openings and Closures

1st February, 1848 - The railway line from St. Ives to March, with intermediate stations at Somersham, Chatteris and Wimblington, opened for freight and for passengers a month later.

16th September, 1889 - Somersham became a junction when the line from Ramsey East to Somersham opened.

30th September 1930 - The Ramsey East to Somersham line closed for passenger trains.

1956 - Goods services were withdrawn between Warboys and Ramsey East.

1964 - Goods services were withdrawn between Somersham and Warboys.

April 1966 - Goods services were withdrawn from the St. Ives – March line.

March 1967 - There was complete closure of the St. Ives – March line and much of the track was removed.

The Bridge over the road

The metal railway bridge crossing the Chatteris Road provided a subway through which most vehicles except very tall ones could pass. Occasionally a high vehicle would try the subway with spectacular results. There was only 9ft 3in (2.8 metres) clearance.

Cyril Gotobed who spent ten years as a signalman at Somersham

A tall van gets stuck under the bridge

recalled some memories of his time working at the station.

"In one such incident a van was travelling from Chatteris and got jammed under the bridge. The driver told me that there was no sign depicting the road clearance on the approach side although there was one on the Somersham side. The driver was very upset, afraid that he would lose his job; this was his third incident in as many months. Out of curiosity I had photographed the incident from both sides of the bridge and feeling rather sorry for the poor fellow I sent a copy of each to his firm. In reply they thanked me for doing so and told me that the evidence provided by the photographs persuaded them not to dismiss the driver. That was very rewarding, as also was the box of their products which arrived a few days later. Another driver tried to creep under the bridge with an empty cattle truck and got well and truly wedged. To add to his misfortunes his lady passenger was not his wife. I couldn't help him out of that one."

SCHOOLS AND EDUCATION

Education in Huntingdonshire was on a very piecemeal basis prior to the reforms of the 19th century. Village schools have been recorded as far back as the 16th century but they were usually of a very temporary nature relying on one educated person who would usually be the local clergyman. The earliest record of a schoolmaster in Somersham is that of Tomas Townsend in 1656 who was appointed as Parish Registrar of Somersham.

In 1712 the Church Curate Rev. Daniel Whiston provided tuition in St. John's Church for a small school of six children. It seems that a thriving Sunday school was in existence by 1717 with sixty five children being instructed by the curate.

The first comprehensive list still surviving of elementary schools appears in Thomas Cox's History of Huntingdonshire and names eighteen charity schools, including one in Somersham, a comparatively large number for a small county. The Somersham Charity School had six poor children who were taught at the expense of the Rector.

The village had its own library by 1746 which was kept at Somersham School. Charity schools relied upon local landowners and other wealthy patrons for their funds as well as on endowments from individuals' wills. The school building in Church Street arose out of a bequest of £200 to the Poor of the Parish of Somersham, from the will of Thomas Hammond Esq. dated 25th December 1746. Unfortunately he did not make it clear how the money was to be spent and for many years legal wrangles went on before it could be put to good use, but the Rev. Whiston was very clear on how this should be done.

On 1st August 1755 Daniel Whiston made an oath in Chancery stating *"That he has been Curate of Somersham aforesaid forty-five years and upwards and was during that time intimately acquainted with Thomas Hammond and that he has heard during this time Thomas Hammond several times affirm he would at his death leave a handsome legacy for the endowment of a Charity School at Somersham."* Nothing else seems to have happened until 21st November 1771 other than the appointment of John Crane, a schoolmaster, on 14th April 1769. It is not clear whether the school was held in the church or another building. Unfortunately Crane died of consumption (T.B.) at the young age of 31.

In 1771 the Trustees finally purchased a site in Church Lane (now Church Street) from the Duke of Manchester for the sum of £4. 14s. 6d. on which to erect a School-room and Master's residence. It would seem that the building was not started for a number of years because the engraved stone above the door

states that it was erected in 1782. John Briggs was appointed Master in 1773 but he was dismissed on the 13th May 1795, to be succeeded by the Rev. Thomas Wilson who resigned on the following Lady Day (25th March).

On the 17th March 1796 a Trustee Meeting of the Charity School started off in the church but soon adjourned to the Rose and Crown Inn. It was unanimously decided that £5 a year should be deducted from the income of the school for the purpose of being paid to some proper person to teach twelve poor children their letters. Also on that day the Rev. John Oakley was appointed Master but he was dismissed in 1799.

The following years were more settled with the appointment on the 2nd January 1800 of Thomas Orbell, of Linton, Cambridgeshire as Master of the school. He was to be the Master for the next forty years. In 1831 the Master received about £25 a year for teaching the three R's to twenty eight boys. A Mistress, whose salary was £5 a year, taught twelve smaller children to read in preparation for admission to the free school. Orbell was succeeded by George Ashley who was dismissed on 4th February 1844.

The trade directories for Somersham show that there were other educational establishments in the village. In 1830 William Orriss, who appears to have been the Baptist Minister, was running a boys' school and Rachael Smith was running a girls' school. In 1839 Philos Gisburne had a Gentlemen's Commercial Academy for boarding and day pupils, in the 1841 Census there were twelve boys between the ages of 8 and 15 in residence. It still appeared in the directories until 1848, but Gisburne is not recorded in the 1851 Census. The Misses Ann and Harriet Pocock ran a Ladies Seminary for boarding and day pupils in the High Street, until at least 1857. In the 1851 census the school is shown as having seven pupils in residence between the ages of 7 and 18 with two teachers.

In 1844 the Charity School was transferred to the Huntingdonshire Board of Education and became the Charity and National School and the school building was enlarged by adding a new wing. The dimensions of the old school were 26 feet by 15 feet. The new wing stretched westward 30 feet by 22 feet. A grant of £40 was given by the Board of Education towards enlarging the school, the remaining sum of £53 being raised by subscriptions.

John William Flack was the Master of the Charity and National School in 1847 and his wife was the Mistress but they left at Christmas 1850 and were succeeded by Joseph Stevens as the Master and his sister-in-law Miss Maria Reed, Mistress; they held the appointment for only one year. Joseph Wright and Mrs. Mary Hempstead were schoolmaster and schoolmistress of private schools as well as the Misses Wilson who also ran a day school, the other schools from 1839 still being in existence. The Post Office directory also notes that there were two Sunday schools at St. John's Church and the Baptist Church.

On the 13th January 1852 William Attfield was appointed the Master of the Charity and National School, and his wife Hannah the Mistress. They stayed at the school for twenty one years before resigning at Christmas 1873.

In James Hatfield's History Gazetteer and Directory of the County of Huntingdon in 1854 it states *"The school house is a good building of red brick; the school-room large, lofty, well lighted and ventilated. It adjoins the churchyard. There are in Somersham well conducted Sunday-schools connected with the several places of worship."* And also *"Under the present system the Master receives a small weekly payment with each child, and has likewise the privilege of instructing other paying scholars. The average attendance of children is about 80."*

Tollington House where the Miss Pococks ran a school

Craven's Directory for 1855 lists Harriet Pocock at the boarding and day school in the High Street, but also Rhoda Clark and Elizabeth Parker are both listed as 'day school, High Street'. Slater's Directory 1857 lists Harriet Wilson as being in charge of a day school and only Ann Pocock is recorded for the boarding and day school.

The Rector allowed the large yard attached to the Tithe Barn to be converted into a playground for the children of the school in 1858. At the same time the ancient Buck Well was restored and the springs used as a bathing place. The library was still located in the Charity and National School.

The 1861 Census shows that Miss Elizabeth Johnson was running a Ladies School at the Manor Hall. However, by the time of the 1871 Census she had married and become Elizabeth Woodroffe but was still shown running the school at the Manor Hall in both the 1871 and 1881 censuses. The school had a number of scholars who were residents and there may have been day pupils.

In 1870 Forster's Elementary Education Act was passed. The Charity and National School in Somersham was found to be 'neither sufficient nor efficient within the meaning of the 1870 Act'. The former defect was remedied by the erection of a classroom to the mixed school, and the building of a new infant school; and the latter by engaging certificated teachers, and pupil teachers. So at Christmas 1873 Nathan Dews was appointed Master of the mixed school. There was another extension to the school grounds, other land at the back of the school was leased by a William Mason from Mrs. Moseley and then donated to the school as a recreation ground. Barns and outbuildings on the plot were removed and a wall was placed around it for the children's safety.

Education finally became compulsory in 1880. Also that year Nathan Dews published his 'History of Somersham'. The Preface of the book states that the main object of compiling the work is that: *"The scholars should show special knowledge of any historical events or characters connected with the district in which their school is situated."* In January Miss Selina Roberts was employed as the Infants Mistress at the school.

Both the Mixed school and Infant schools were then known as Public Elementary Schools fulfilling all of the requirements of the Education Department. The school property was conveyed to trustees who had various powers given to them for the management and government of the school. Nathan Dews left the school in 1879 and Charles Nettleship White became the new Master.

In 1885 there was communication between the Education Department and the School Trustees and after various discussions and some prolonged 'wordy warfare' in the local newspapers, it was decided to form a School Board. An election was held and the five candidates with the most votes were elected.

In 1876 the Harrod's Directory records that Miss Hempsted, Miss Ibbott and Mrs. Woodroffe ran Mixed Middle Class schools and that Mrs. Harriet Holdich ran a Ladies School. However, she was assisted by her sister Mrs. Betsy Frampton and her niece Clara Frampton who were teachers at the school. Kelly's Directory for 1898 records for the first time that Mrs. Betsy Frampton was running a private school for girls. This was at Ivy Cottage (at the site of the present Ivy House in the High Street). Amazingly she was about 78 years of age and her daughter Clara was 35 years old. Successive directories show that Betsy continued to run the school until at least 1914, but the 1920 directory shows that the school was run by Miss Clara Frampton and in 1928 was taking boys and girls. The school's last entry was in 1931.

In 1901 the Infants School was built in Church Street (the building is the present Community Information Centre) with enough places for one hundred and ten children! Ernest Arthur Edwards, who was born on 15th October 1895 in Church Lane, recalling his memories of Somersham in jottings written when he was 83 years old, said:

"I went to school at 3 years of age in the Old School before the Infants was built opposite. We were lined in the Lane, I

The Infants School

remember the march down from the top school to the new school, I should be about 5 years of age then, but I can't remember the three old Stud and Mud houses with thatch roof on them there before the school was built. My Grandmother Edwards lived in one. Old lady Gowler and a man name Sutton lived in the others. From the infant school we came back to the top school about six years of age. I can't remember much of what we learnt only read and write but left school at 11 year of age and started work down the Fens from 7 o'clock till 4 pm for 6d a day". (2½ pence today).

School Boards were abolished in 1902 and the supervision of elementary education was taken over by the new County Councils. Kelly's Directory of 1898 shows that Edward Parkinson was the Master of the Board School, formerly known as the National School, which had an average attendance of one hundred boys and girls and sixty five infants. The school had enough places for two hundred and fifty pupils.

At the beginning of the Second World War in 1939 there was an influx of children to Somersham who had been evacuated from North London. It was decided that local children would attend school from 8.30 - 12.30 pm and the evacuated children attend from 1.15 - 5.15 pm.

The 1944 Education Act came into operation in April of that year, and laid down that all children were to pass from the primary to the secondary stage of education at the age of 11-12 years. On 7th June the following year the school buildings in Church Street were surveyed and photographed as part of the County Development Plan. There were four classrooms in the mixed senior school plus three cloakrooms. It was heated by four stoves and had gas lighting and mains water. Two male and one female teacher were employed to teach one hundred and five pupils. On the 10th June the Infant school was also surveyed, it had two classrooms.

At the end of April 1964 the school moved to new premises in Parkhall Road. A headline in the Hunts Post read *"Pioneer Somersham school opened - it replaces a building condemned in 1926"*. At the formal opening visitors and pupils were told that *"their patience had been rewarded with a school that is quite a pioneer school and unique in many particulars and that there were not many schools in the country with such facilities"*.

A former pupil remembers that most of the books and other school resources were moved from the old buildings to the new one by the children themselves who made a good number of trips up Church Street to the new school and back again. Mr. Taylor was the Headmaster at that time. He retired in July 1973 and Mr. Philip Clarke was appointed as the new Headmaster of Somersham County Primary School. In those days teachers often taught in the same school for most of their working lives.

In 1975 Miss Few retired after teaching in Somersham for forty one years and in 1978 Miss Brown retired after forty years with the local authority. Her last two appointments were as Acting Head at the closure of Pidley School and then at Somersham School. Mrs. Helen Cole who was appointed to take Miss Brown's place, retired in 2008 having taught in the school for thirty years.

The Whitehall School, an independent primary, was opened in 1983 at 117 High Street continuing a long tradition of private schooling in the village since at least the 1830s.

There are two playgroups for pre-school age children. Parkhall Playgroup started in the Wesleyan chapel in Parkhall Road but moved to a mobile classroom on the school site in November 1984. This was demolished in 2010 and Cambridgeshire County Council funded the building of a Children's Centre on the site. The playgroup moved into part of the new building in August 2011. The First Steps Playgroup meets in the Scout Hut on the Norwood playing fields.

In 1985 The Rev. Arthur Ludlow (Rector) asked Mary Baker if she would help restart St. John's Young Church in what was the old Infants School. Twenty three years later she was still there organising it. After various homes it unfortunately had to fold in March 2007 due mainly to a lack of a suitable venue.

SHOPS

There are very few shops in Somersham today but before the advent of supermarkets and the widespread ownership of cars people had to do most of their shopping in the village. There were a lot more shops including several bakers and butchers, two banks (Barclays and Lloyds) and even a jewellers shop. The shops were not just in the High Street, but also in Rectory Lane and along 'The Bank'.

These are some of the shops that have served the village the longest.

The Department Store

Charles Norman & Son,
SOMERSHAM.

Phone: SOMERSHAM 15.

High Class Grocers, Drapers, Furnishers, and General Warehousemen.

An advertisement from a 1936 Church Parish Magazine

MAIN DEPARTMENTS—

LADIES' AND GENTS' TAILORING (Mourning orders supplied in 24 hours)
HOUSE FURNISHING (Throughout).
MILLINERY, MANTLES, GOWNS,
LADIES' GENTS' AND CHILDREN'S BOOTS, SHOES AND WELLINGTONS, Etc.
FLOOR FURNISHINGS.
CARPETS, RUGS, COCO MATTING AND LINOLEUMS (Printed and Inlaid).

New Showroom for China, Glass, Pyrex and Aluminium Ware.

Stockists of—
"Ewbank" Sweepers and Mangles.
"Darling" Washers and "Acme" Wringers.

Agents for—
"Mascot" and "Norvic" Brands Boots and Shoes.
Also "Sol" and "Bolko" Prams and Baby Cars.

"ALADDIN" LAMPS.
"E:E:E:E:" (For Ease) THE Superchair. Fireside Chairs.
Men's "Dryfoot" Boots for really dry feet.

Our extensive range of Furniture, Carpets, etc., may be viewed in complete privacy at our newly acquired ASSEMBLY HALL SHOWROOM.

ALL GOODS ARE MARKED IN PLAIN FIGURES.

Customers at a distance will find it a distinct advantage that when delivering we can include goods from so many departments.

Charles Norman & Son was the village's own department store from 1902 until 1972. The advertisement on the previous page from a 1936 Church Parish magazine gives an indication of the range of goods that were for sale.

The main shop was on the corner of Parkhall Road and the men's outfitters were in the adjoining building in the High Street. The furnishing department was in a building next to the George Inn. They also had a furniture store at the Assembly Room (next to the old Tithe Barn).

Norman's Main Shop

The Baker Shop
The oldest established family business in Somersham was, until May 2013, **Bonnett's** the baker shop which had been baking bread, cakes and pastries in Somersham since 1803. Each successive generation of the Bonnett family has been told that their family were Huguenots who had arrived in England during

130

the French Revolution in the 1790s. David Bonnett has written evidence that William Bonnett owned a baker shop in Somersham in 1803, but he believes the bakery had been established sometime before that date. Until it closed five generations had been involved in the everyday running of the bakery.

Bonnett's Shop

William Bonnett, also known as Newman Bonnett, ran the business until he died in 1880 at the age of sixty-three. He was followed by his son William Newman.   **William Newman Bonnett** died in 1912 at the age of seventy-one, at which time his son William was thirty-one. William died in 1918 at the age of thirty-seven and his wife Bessie took over.

Bessie Bonnett ran the business with the help of her sons Sidney and Fred and her daughter Irene and they all lived above the shop until 1946. They then moved to the Chestnuts, the large Georgian style house (now called Mulberry House) next to the shop. Bessie's head baker was a man called Billie Barlow, and some people in the village still remember a saying that he used in her day: "Bessie Bonnett's best-baked brown bread, baked by Billie Barlow, builds bonny babies". Bessie was a good business woman and ran the business for twenty eight years until she handed it over to her two sons and daughter. She died in 1955 at the age of 70.

During that time Bonnett's flourished with more customers and set up shops in Chatteris and Earith and later in other towns and villages. Door-to-door deliveries in the village were made on foot whilst those further afield were made using a horse and cart.

Later three-wheeled cycles were used – one of which remained in use for many years for special deliveries and sales of hot cross buns on Good Friday. Motor vehicles were introduced in the 1920s and a 1954 Ford 10 van, painted in the company's original colours of cream and green, was still used to make deliveries on special occasions until the shop closed.

One of the Bonnett's vans and one of the tricycles

Sidney Bonnett went into the army in the Second World War, where he was a cook until he was demobbed in 1946. Then

Sidney, along with his brother Fred and sister Irene, ran the business until 1979 and three years later he died suddenly in 1982 at the age of sixty six.

David Bonnett took over from his father and ran the business until he retired in 2013 and with no family member wishing to continue it the shop closed.

The Sweet Shop

Miss Ball outside the Sweet Shop

It was the end of an era in June 1988, when a shop in the High Street, which had been serving sweets to local youngsters since the 1800s, closed. The former shopkeeper, 90-year-old Miss Hilda Ball had died and there was no-one to keep the shop, which had been in the family for several generations.

The ownership of the shop has been traced back to a William

Ball, who died at the age of 93, and who apprenticed as a bootmaker in the shop which he later came to own. He lived in the village all his life, apart from a short time, when he made boots for the army in Northampton during the Crimean War. The shop was then handed down to his daughter, Miss Eliza Ball, who later became Mrs. Eliza Elmore. She ran the shop for fifty years and died at the age of 80, leaving it to her daughter Miss May Elmore and niece Miss Hilda Ball.

May Elmore was well known by villagers for giving packets of cigarettes to servicemen throughout the Second World War. At Christmastime there were toys at the back of the shop and the children used to love to go in and see them.

The Chemists
There has been a local chemist offering services to the inhabitants of the Somersham area since the 1850s and No. 83 High Street (Galen House) has had continuous occupation by a chemist's shop for at least one hundred and thirty five years!

The first recorded chemist in the village was **Charles Bayes**. In the 1851 census he was aged 33 and in business as a chemist and druggist in Somersham. He had been born in Kettering, Northamptonshire, and ten years earlier, in 1841, had been a chemist in Market Hill, Kettering. Since then he had married; his daughter had been born in Kettering in about 1848/9; and the family had moved to Somersham. They lived at 52 High Street, Somersham. By 1861 Charles had ceased to be a chemist and had returned to Kettering and appeared to be running the family farm.

In the 1854 Post Office Directory there is an entry for Somersham of **Edward Sanderson**, chemist. However, in Hatfield's History, Gazetteer and Directory of the County of

Huntingdon for 1854, a **Mary Sanderson** was listed as the chemist and druggist in Somersham. This may be the Mary Sanderson who in the 1841-1891 censuses was based in North Street, Crowland, Lincolnshire. She was married to William Sanderson who was a chemist. It would appear that for some reason Mary had run the chemist business in Somersham around the year 1854, perhaps on a temporary basis.

The 1855 volume of Craven's Commercial Directory of the County of Huntingdon entered **Ambrose Wray Warden** as chemist and druggist in the High Street, Somersham. In the 1851 census Ambrose, aged 22, had been staying with his grandfather, John Wray, Vicar of Bardney, Lincolnshire, and was a druggist apprentice to his uncle, William Henry Wray, druggist in Bardney. By 1861 Ambrose had left Somersham and was a chemist in Hackney.

In the 1861 census **William Brown** was the Chemist and Druggist in the village. He was aged 57 and was married to Mary Ann Brown and they had four children. He also had a servant who was listed as a chemist. They lived on the south side of Main Street (later known as High Street), two properties away from the Crown and Punch Bowl public house. On 23rd September he filed a notice of bankruptcy which was published in the London Gazette. In the 1871 Battersea census Mary Ann was listed as a widow, so William must have died.

A notice of bankruptcy identified another chemist of Somersham named **Daniel Burgess**. In 1861, Daniel, aged 28, was in business as a chemist in Sydenham, Kent where he lived with his wife, Emma Clarissa, and two children. He then moved to Somersham but his address is not known. On 14th November 1862 there was an item published in the London Gazette stating that Daniel Burgess, formerly of Sydenham but now of

Somersham, Huntingdonshire, had been adjudged bankrupt. This was followed by a report that his discharge was to be considered at the Court of Bankruptcy on 8th January 1863. Nearly twenty years later, in the 1881 census Daniel was continuing to work as a chemist, living with his wife in Tower Hamlets.

Joseph Lavender was the village chemist and druggist in the 1871 census. He was aged 39 and was residing with his wife Matilda and four children in Somersham Main Street. Ten years earlier, he had appeared in the 1861 census as a chemist and druggist/shopman in Back Street, Chatteris, his home town. Joseph and Matilda's third child was born in Somersham c1866, which suggested that the family moved to Somersham between 1861 and 1866.

A couple of years after Mr. Lavender set up business in Somersham, the 1868 Pharmacy Act was passed. Its aim was to regulate the sales of poisons and to protect the public by requiring persons, who sold, dispensed or compounded poisons, to register as chemists and druggists with the Pharmaceutical Society. After this date, qualification by examination was a requirement. The Pharmaceutical Society Register of Chemists and Druggists recorded that Joseph Lavender was registered on 31st December 1868 in the category of 'in business before 1st August 1868'. The earliest Pharmaceutical Society Register which can be accessed is dated 1880 and Mr. Lavender was no longer living in Somersham.

The next chemist was **Joshua Goodenough.** He was born on 20th April 1848 and his father was a farmer in Town End, March. He qualified as a chemist and druggist by examination and was registered by the Pharmaceutical Society on 15th June 1870. The entry in the 1871 census indicated that he was employed as a chemist's assistant and resided as a lodger in Pottergate, Norwich.

J. GOODENOUGH,
CHEMIST & DRUGGIST,
SOMERSHAM

Is prepared to dispense Physicians' Prescriptions, and to supply genuine Drugs and Chemicals, and all Patent and Proprietary Medicines.

Cough Mixture, 1/- per bottle.
Quinine & Iron Tonic, 1/- per bottle.
Bilious & Liver Pills, 1/- per box.
Cod Liver Oil Emulsion, 1/- per bottle.
Household Ammonia, 1/-
Universal Embrocation, 1/-

TOOTH BRUSHES, SPONGES, TOILET SOAPS. PERFUMES.

GOODENOUGH'S AERATED WATERS, 9d. per doz.

HORSE and CATTLE MEDICINES.

PHOTOGRAPHIC DRY PLATES, PRINTING PAPERS and FRAMES, DEVELOPING and FIXING SOLUTIONS.

Petroleum (Water White), Lamps, Wicks, & Glasses.

An Advertisement from a 1908 Church Parish Magazine

Joshua had an entry as the Somersham chemist and druggist in an 1876 trade directory. The 1881 census recorded that Mr. Goodenough, aged 32, chemist and druggist, lived with his wife, Millicent, of St. Ives, and three children in High Street, Somersham. The eldest child was born in Somersham in 1875/6. The census listings appear to suggest that they occupied No. 83 High Street. Therefore it appears that he moved to Somersham between 1871 and 1876. Sources of information do not clarify whether he took over the business premises of Joseph Lavender or whether Mr. Lavender had moved to No. 83 High Street before going to Leicester.

In an 1890 trade directory for Somersham, Joshua Goodenough was listed as both a chemist and aerated water manufacturer and this was repeated in the 1910 and 1914 Kelly's Directory of Huntingdonshire.

Aerated water was one of the most popular drinks during the Victorian period. People had taken natural mineral waters for their healing powers for hundreds of years and then scientists discovered how to produce and bottle carbonated 'aerated' water. Goodenough manufactured the drink in buildings behind the shop. An early 1900s Ordnance Survey Map showed a long building to the rear and a remaining part of the outbuilding was shown in a 1970s aerial photograph. Later occupants of the chemist shop, the Morgans, talked of the fun of finding marbles, once used as bottle stoppers, in the garden. Joshua Goodenough later moved to 'Homeleigh', (a name given to half of the Manor Hall), Parkhall Road. He retired in 1920 and died on 15th April 1931. He is buried in Somersham Parish Churchyard and a short obituary which was published in the Hunts Post records that he was well known, highly respected, a prominent churchman and former school manager.

Henry Jones Morgan was the next chemist in the village. He moved from a pharmacy in Kimbolton to Somersham in 1920, with his wife, Edith, of Bicester, and two children, Ivan and Olwen. Mr. Morgan was born in Pembrokeshire on 24th December 1880. He was educated at Haverfordwest Grammar School; undertook a chemist and druggist apprenticeship in Narberth, Pembrokeshire; and was a chemist's assistant in Bicester, Oxfordshire. He qualified by examination and was registered by the Pharmaceutical Society on 25th September 1909.

Henry Morgan also provided dental services. Pharmacists performing such work before 1921 could apply for inclusion on the Register of Dentists, established in 1878, and Mr. Morgan was registered. After the introduction of the 1921 Dentists Act, entry to the profession was by examination only. However, under this Act, pharmacists, judged as competent, could continue their practice. He also pursued the occupation of optician with enthusiasm and studied for numerous qualifications including the Diploma and the Fellow of the British Optical Association, the Diploma in Ophthalmics (of the Institute of Optical Science) and became a Fellow of the Spectacle Makers Company – which led to him receiving the Freedom of the City of London on 22nd June 1922.

Henry Morgan had a lifelong interest in theology, was a lay preacher and studied the bible. His children attended Miss Frampton's school in Somersham. Henry died on 16th March 1955 and was buried in Somersham Parish Churchyard. An obituary was published in the Hunts Post of 24th March 1955.

A Label from a Medicine Bottle   *Henry Morgan*

Samuel Cyril Barratt took over the chemist business in 1955. He qualified as a pharmacist and was registered by the Pharmaceutical Society on 28th September 1926. His contact address in the 1954 and 1955 Registers was c/o Boots Ltd, High Street, Wisbech, and, in 1956, it was changed to Galen House, High Street, Somersham. This address was retained through to the 1970 Register. In the 1971 volume, Mr. Barratt had retired and his address was given as Station House, Somersham. He died in 1975.

139

John William Anderson arrived as the next pharmacist in February 1970. He was born on 10 April 1936 and registered as a qualified chemist on 24th August 1959. In the mid-1960s he moved from St. Ives to The Causeway, Godmanchester, and, from 1970 onwards, travelled daily to Somersham.

These are examples of his advertisements. The one on the left is from a 1970s Church Parish Magazine and the other is from a 1990s Carnival Magazine. It shows that the shop diversified its trade during John Anderson's time as the chemist in the village.

J. W. ANDERSON	J. W. ANDERSON
B.PHARM., M.P.S.	TOYS • GAMES • BOOKS • GIFTS
DISPENSING CHEMIST	TOILETRIES • COSMETICS • PERFUMES
Proprietary Medicines; Toilet Requisites, Photographic, Agricultural and Horticultural Supplies	BABY REQUISITES
	WATCHES & CLOCKS
	GREETING CARDS & STATIONERY
	SEEDS & GARDEN SUPPLIES
	FILMS DEVELOPING & PRINTING
High St., Somersham	83/85 High St. SODA STREAM AGENT Ramsey
Telephone : Somersham 219	Somersham. 840219

Mr. Anderson retired on 31st October 2000.

140

The Somersham chemist's business was continued by **Tushar Patel**, who was entered in the Register of Pharmaceutical Chemists on 30 July 1992.

In the shop, Mr. Patel found a thick leather bound 'Day Book', which contains a record of dispensing activity from March 1952 to March 1973. The older entries in the tome, dated October 1927 to June 1928, referred to goods sold at the ironmonger's, C. Ashmore and Son of Bicester, the family business of Henry Jones Morgan's in-laws, and covered the period just prior to Charles Ashmore's death. The half used volume had proved to be useful to Mr. Barratt, when he took over from Mr. Morgan.

The Fish and Chip Shop

Reg Manley, Stan Johnson & 'Nudger' Turner outside the bungalow next to Manley's Fish and Chip Shop

Although there was a Fish and Chip Shop at West End for a short time and another one in the High Street, the premises in

Parkhall Road is the longest serving one. It was started in 1922 by Reg Manley. Where the fish shop is now there was another house. It was in a row of three houses and there was a gateway between the house and the shop and then there were two cottages. Reg lived in the bungalow beside the shop. He was 22 when he started the fish shop and is listed in the trade directories as a fried fish dealer. Reg also sold wet fish from the back of the premises. He retired when he was 65 and the shop was then passed to his son Geoff and son-in-law Bern Kimber and they had it for seventeen years. Reg's daughter Ivy, (later to become Bern's wife) started working in the shop when she was 15, at the time the Second World War broke out, and worked there until she was 58. Geoff and Bern gave up the shop in 1982.

Since that time the shop has had a number of owners and suffered mixed fortunes, the business going into decline at times and thriving at others. The shop even had to close for several months to be refitted after a serious fire completely blackened the inside of the premises in 2008.

Garages

Just as there were many shops in Somersham there were quite a few garages. Today the only garage where you can buy petrol is Bridge End Garage, usually known as 'Cole & Days'.

One can get an idea of the businesses that were connected to the motor trade from adverts in old church parish magazines and more recently from the carnival magazines. Walter Brudenell first advertised as a motor and cycle engineer in 1927 and his advertisements continued until at least 1940. As his phone number was Somersham 203 which later appears in 1960 adverts for 'Somersham Motors' and also in 1970 adverts for 'Bridge End Garage' it seems reasonable to assume that they all traded from the same site near the Station Approach end of the High Street.

Phone 203.

WALTER BRUDENELL,

Everything for the Car, Cycle and Radio.

Electric Lamps and Fittings.

District Agent for Raleigh and Humber Cycles.

CARS FOR HIRE.

SOMERSHAM, Huntingdon.

1940 Church Parish Magazine Advertisement

SOMERSHAM MOTORS LTD.

Agricultural, Electrical and Motor Engineers

Body Repairs, Panel-beating and Spraying
CAR HIRE SERVICE for Weddings and Special Occasions
Car Cellulosing, Tyre Dealers, Insurances, Large Stocks Spares
Agents for Drake & Fletcher & Cooper Fruit Spraying Equipment

SOMERSHAM, Huntingdon
Telephone : Somersham 203

1964 Advertisement

Somersham 203

Bridge End Garage

(SOMERSHAM) LTD.
Motor & Agricultural Engineers
New and Secondhand Car Sales
Tractors and Agricultural Machines
HIGH STREET, SOMERSHAM
HUNTS.

1972 Advertisement

Shell Petrol Sign at Brown's

In 1936 Charles Brown also advertised as a motor and cycle engineer. His adverts as a cycle agent continued in the 1940s and 1950s. He traded on the Cross between numbers 91 and 93 High Street and sold Shell petrol from pumps with a hose on an arm which reached out across the pavement. The petrol tanks were installed during the Second World War for use by the army. After the war Mr. Brown then started selling petrol, as well as paraffin, to the general public. Adverts in the 1960s and 70s show that Brown's Garage was owned by Stan Saint. In 1971 it was taken over by Leon Buddle. The District Council was keen to stop garages selling petrol in villages, especially across the pavement, so they pressure tested the petrol tanks and those that failed were prohibited from stocking up with further supplies.

However, the first petrol pump (wind up, not electric) in the village was installed at West End Garage in the 1920s. In the 1950s an electric pump dispensed the 'Cleveland' brand of petrol, and later Esso.

West End Garage was created from four adjoining cottages and was owned by George Dolby. He ran a haulage business and owned a number of steam engines. On the side of the original cottages there is the cycle shop which George also ran, but he never did car repairs. The garage last sold petrol in 1968 but a Cleveland and an Esso pump stood outside the building until

Left: The four adjoining cottages c.1910

Right: West End Garage in 2008

Left: West End Garage in 2013

145

about 2010 when a car showroom was built. When George died and his widow moved to a home on the opposite side of the St. Ives Road, the garage became derelict for several years before the present owner bought it in 1993.

Left: Brooker & Clements at West End
Below: At the corner of Feoffees Road

Car repairs in the village were carried out for many years by Brooker and Clements who had workshops at the end of Feoffees Road. The houses at Brooker's Place partly stand on the site of the garage. Their first advert appeared in 1954 and continued through to the 1970s. Prior to this they had traded from premises which were built on the site of the 1942 air crash.

When Brooker & Clements moved to Feoffees Road the premises were taken over by Hunts TBA (Tyres, Batteries & Accessories) Services, also known as Central Tyres and the garage was eventually demolished and replaced by the buildings called Carpenter's Court.

Above: Carnival Magazine Advertisement 1979

Dews Coaches

Familiar sights in the district are the coaches and buses of Dews Coaches in their distinctive green livery. The firm was established in 1953 by Ron Dew. Having served in the RAF during the war and realising that the family fruit wholesale business would not provide him and his brother-in-law with a living, he started driving lorries and then buses. He bought a 1939 Bedford bus and started the business, operating from Norfolk House (52 High Street) which was owned by his father-in-law, Walter Aubrey.

A significant development for the company occurred when St. Ivo School opened in 1954. Ron applied for, and won, the contract to run their school buses.

Ron's son David started working for the company when he was 21 following his apprenticeship in commercial maintenance, passing his PSV test to drive and maintain the coaches. In the

The 1939 Bedford bus with which Ron Dew started the business

mid-sixties the firm won contracts with blue chip companies such as Pye Telecommunications in Cambridge and Sinclair in St. Ives to transport its employees to and from work. These contracts also led to more work from Cambridgeshire County Council Education Transport Department to operate additional school buses. Smart new green and grey coaches were bought and sold during the years and became a symbol of quality and stylish travel.

148

In 1971, when Dews took their first coach trip abroad travelling to Interlaken with the Ailwyn School, Ramsey, David recalls that there was only one other coach on the ferry across the Channel. With a little more expansion and the advent of larger, longer coaches seating more passengers, a larger premises was required. In that year Ron & David also bought and moved to the yard in Parkhall Road when Huckles, a firm of Corn Merchants, who had been the village's largest employers, closed. At that time they had about five coaches.

Dew's Coach Yard in Parkhall Road

During 1978 David and Linda decided to branch out into their own tour programme taking passengers mainly to European destinations such as Boppard in Germany and Kandersteg in Switzerland where the family formed close bonds with family hotels still used and enjoyed today. The name chosen was Dewsway Tours. Many local well known families travelled with the company until around 1992.

149

David's son Simon joined the family business in 1989 and once again another expansion led to a further move, this time to their current location along Chatteris Road. The site was spotted and although it took eighteen months to achieve the necessary planning permission, they moved to this site on the eastern edge of the village in February 1991 with about ten coaches.

Simon bought new ideas that helped the company expand further. Simon bought his first coach for the business in 1993 and has never looked back, and now, with Linda and David's retirement, runs the family firm with his wife Debbie. Dews Coaches currently operate seven touring coaches and twenty two school buses as well as five vintage coaches. On a regular basis they have had some prestigious contracts including transporting NATO representatives and international rugby teams every year since 1997, these include New Zealand, Australia, South Africa and Argentina. In 2012 Dews Coaches won the very important contract to transport the corporate clients of Coca Cola during the Olympics in London. They are almost certainly one of, if not, the largest employers in the village having forty four people on their payroll.

There had been other coach firms in the village. Charlie Margo ran a business in Somersham from about 1943 called Margo's Transport. He had about ten Coaches and ten Lorries. He carried men to work on the airfields and also transported cement. Later he took the P.O.W.s (Prisoners of War) to do agricultural work. He parked the vehicles on the site of the air crash next to the White Lion pub and when the P.O.Ws left he had a big airplane hanger constructed on the site where the P.O.Ws were billeted in camps by the Rectory. His daughter says that when Ron Dew came out of the army Charlie Margo helped teach him to drive a coach.

PUBLIC HOUSES

Today there are only three public houses in Somersham; The George, The Rose and Crown and The Windmill, but once there were many more.

It is said that there were over thirty Public Houses in the Parish of Somersham. These are the names of the pubs that are no long trading, that I have found recorded in various archives, such as Kelly's Directories.

Using the census records it is possible to find where they were located.

In the High Street

No. 2. **The Rising Sun** (on the corner of Colne Road opposite the garage – still trading in 1940).

No. 23. **The Brewers Arms** (now called Fairway).

No. 26. **The Railway Inn** and **The Prince of Wales** appear to have been the same building with alternating names between the 1861, 1871, 1881 and 1891 censuses (still trading in 1930) and more recently may have been known as **The Drum & Monkey** – a building no longer in existence.

No 42. **The Crown & Punch Bowl** (still trading in 1910).

No 58. **The Lion** (in the 1881 census it is the **Lion and Lamb** although in other censuses it is just the Lion) .

No 71. **The Six Bells** (next to Wisteria House – still

trading in 1930). Previous to 1782 the Parish Church only had five bells so this pub probably started trading later than that date.

No. 86. **The Horse & Jockey** is recorded in the 1861 Census

No 89. **The Black Bull** in the censuses prior to 1891 this pub was known as 'The Bull' and there is evidence that it was in existence in 1671 (closed in 2011).

No 111. **The Hammer & Anvil** in the 1891 census seems to show that this pub was formerly called 'The Blacksmith's Arms (closed in 1950).

No 121. **The Carpenter's Arms** (next to the The King William the Fourth and destroyed by the 1942 air crash).

No 123. **The King William the Fourth** (next to the White Lion and destroyed by the 1942 air crash).

No 125. **The White Lion** (still open in 1940)

The Red Cow was in the centre of the village in an area known as Red Cow Hill which could have been a small cul de sac on the south side of the High Street (it was supposedly burnt down in 1857, but appeared in the 1861 and 1871 censuses).

Church Street (formerly Church Lane)

> **The Blacksmith's Arms** (on the east side of the street in the 1861 and 1871 censuses and not far from the Cross).

Parkhall Road

> **Drove House** (opposite the Victory Hall – still trading in 1940).

The Bank

On the Colnefields side of the road -

> **The Queen's Head** – 3 houses along (closed in 1972)
>
> **The Durham Ox** – 8 houses along
>
> **The Queen Victoria** – 20 houses along.

On the opposite side of the road –

> **The Wagon & Horses** (the last house before Dews Coach Yard – still trading in 1940).

Outside the Village

The Wheat Sheaf, also known as Heath House (St. Ives Road/Woodhurst to Bluntisham Crossroad) ceased trading in 1920.

The Three Horseshoes (occurs in the 1861 Census on the Chatteris Road just before the Chatteris Toll)

The children of William Green (publican) standing outside the Plum Tree.

The sign board is on the post at the left of the building

The Plum Tree (on the Chatteris Road just before the Chatteris Toll).

The Blue Ball (at Chatteris Toll, probably not in the Parish of Somersham, later renamed the **Crafty Fox**).

The Spade & Beckett (out on the edge of the Fen on Fenton Lode) possibly the Public House that was recorded in the 1891 Census as sign unknown. It is marked on one of the old ordnance survey maps.

John W. Baker, who was the landlord of the Queen's Head, Somersham until its closure in 1972 gave some fascinating insights into what the pubs were like.

Below: The house that was once the 'Queen's Head'.
Inset: The sign on the cottage showing its name as a public house.

"Many of them would not be as we regard public houses today, they were ordinary dwelling houses where beer was sold and some are actually marked on old maps with BH (Beer House), they had no bar and no pumps, the beer was served directly from wooden barrels.   At one time four out of the twenty five houses along the Bank were beer houses.

Practically all licensees had a second occupation, besides running a pub. Generally they worked in agriculture but also there was a miller, baker, house painter, cobbler and a blacksmith. Years ago pubs were recognised focal points for discussion of every conceivable subject, the favourite being ones occupation, nearly everyone taking a great pride in their work, which was largely executed by hand, there being no labour saving mechanical aids at that time.

At harvest times several workers would call each morning to take a gallon or half gallon jug of beer to work, leaving the empty jug on their return at night ready for filling the following morning. There were no permitted hours for serving beer so the pubs were open from 6 am to 10 pm. Most pubs had a slate on which was registered the amount of beer certain customers had during the week and it was rubbed clean upon payment of the amount owing at the end of the week.

Beer was delivered by horse drawn drays from local breweries such as Lindsalls at Chatteris, Jenkins & Jones and Marshall Brothers at Huntingdon, Cutlack and Harlock of Ely, Bailey & Tebbutt and Dales of Cambridge. All of theses breweries ceased trading long ago or were taken over by larger regional or national breweries. Each drayman was allowed one gallon of beer per day, this being carried in a stone container gently swinging from the rear of the dray as the horses jogged along."

John's father and grandfather were licensees of the Queen's Head which first became his home in 1921 when beer was 4d per pint and cigarettes were 4d for ten.

PAST LIFE IN SOMERSHAM

The Fairs
There was also, for many years a summer fair which was held on the feast of St John the Baptist, the patron saint of the Church and a winter fair on the Friday before the 22nd November for "peddlery and small ware". The right to hold the fairs at Somersham were granted to the Bishop of Ely in 1320.

On the reverse side of the old photograph below the following is written *"June 1908 If the man on the left had not paid to put this rubbish on the Cross* (just to keep the Fair open) *the Charter would have be lost, & the Fair done away with. EKG."* It is believed that the men are Ben Aspinall (Chimney Sweep), Bob Lowe and George Chapman.

Benefit or Friendly Societies
At one time there was no government assistance when workers were sick or died so people would join mutual aid organisations

known as benefit or friendly societies which were established to help families against hardship brought about by illness or death. In Somersham one such an organisation was the "Loyal Order of Ancient Shepherds" ("loyal" referring to the Crown and "shepherds" to the Nativity of Jesus) which had two lodges in the village. One was called the "Shepherd's Pasture Lodge" and met at the Rose & Crown and the other was the "Charity Lodge" and met at the Crown & Punchbowl. The members carried a shepherd's crook in processions and they had a very fine banner.

In May 1875 Shepherds Pasture Lodge had 167 members and the Charity Lodge had 121 members. The benefits offered were 10 shillings per week with the attendance of a doctor in the case of sickness and £10 on the death of a member. Its objects were *"to relieve the sick, bury the dead, and assist each other in all cases of unavoidable distress, so far as in our power lies, and for the promotion of peace and goodwill towards the human race"*.

The Shepherds marching on a 'Hospital Sunday' parade — the boys are carrying their shepherd's crooks

158

Today it exists as the Shepherd's Friendly Society and has greatly extended its original brief. The Shepherds once owned the land we now know as 'The Pastures', as well as 'Shepherds Terrace'. The name 'Shepherds Pasture' was suggested when the naming of the development was considered so as to keep the name of the ancient order alive. However, there was concern that there would be confusion with Shepherds Terrace so it was simplified to 'The Pasture'.

Royal Visitors to Somersham - 1334 to 1605

The presence of the Bishop's Palace and the hunting in the surrounding woods attracted a number of royal visits over the years 1334 to 1605. The following monarchs are known to have visited the village by virtue of letters signed in Somersham.

Close roll letters (so called because registered copies of private letters were closed with a seal) were signed at Somersham by King Edward III on 11th April 1334. He also signed Patent Rolls (registered copies of Letters Patent) there the next day.

King Richard II visited at least three times signing Close Rolls in Somersham on 18th July 1387 and again on 16th May 1393 and 20th March 1399.

King Henry VII signed Patent Rolls at Somersham on 30th August 1486.

King James I wrote a letter to Sir John Cutts (Keeper of Somersham Chace) from which it can be deduced that he had visited Somersham when Cutts was not present because of sickness. The gist of the letter was that the king liked the place but was not pleased that it had been run down, and as he wanted to hunt there in the future, asked Cutts to restock the Chace with deer from Cutt's own herds, or those of his neighbours, so that he could hunt there the next summer. He also asked that a 'careful' gamekeeper be appointed.

Somersham Spa

On the Ordnance Survey Map of Huntingdon and Peterborough (Sheet 142) is a place called Bathe Hill on the St.Ives to Somersham Road (B1040). It was near here that the famous Somersham Spring Waters, commonly known as the Somersham Spa, ran.

Somersham was one of the first mineral springs to develop into a cure centre and to bottle its product for public consumption. There is no record of when this mineral spring was first discovered but the waters were being drunk at the end of the 17th century, then apparently the springs became neglected. In about 1720 they were revived. The water was bottled and corked, then sold as far away as Lincolnshire, Norfolk and even London. It was taken medicinally and mixed with wine.

Somersham became a centre that brought benefit to most of the surrounding villages. People with ailments stayed in the area for the whole summer 'to take the waters'. Then a report was spread that the waters were harmful and consequently the spring eventually became unused and totally neglected. The buildings became derelict and were demolished.

A London Physician, Dr. Layard, who had spent twelve years practicing in Huntingdon, tried to renew the reputation of the waters. He published a pamphlet on the Somersham Spring in 1759 and a second edition in 1767, which was really an advertisement. The virtue of the water didn't really catch on and all records of the spring fade out before the 19th century. The well to the spring has now been filled in and no one would ever know it had been there.

Although it was always known as Somersham Spa it was actually in the Parish of Woodhurst.

The Pageant and the Mystery Play
In the late nineteenth and early twentieth centuries historic pageants were very popular. One man was particularly associated with the staging of such events; his name was D'Arcy de Ferrars. Most pageants took place in cities and large towns. So when in 1908 a pageant was mounted in Somersham it was quite extraordinary, so much so that one of the leading London newspapers sent a reporter from the capital to write about the event. The director of the pageant was D'Arcy de Ferrars. So how did he get involved? Well the answer is that the Vicar at that time, the Rev. Magens de Courcy-Ireland, was the cousin of D'Arcy's wife.

The Vicar was keen to stage a pageant in Somersham and received the support of his parishioners. The preparations were first mentioned in the parish magazine of July 1908. *"The*

various Committees are hard at work and sparing no pains to make the production as artistic and accurate as possible, the Choruses are learning their parts and the Costume Making will soon be in full swing."

Maypole Dance

It was to be a village display in the form of tableaux representing various historical episodes with local connections. The intention was to hold it in the autumn but it was moved forward to 10-12th August, so there were only about three weeks for planning and rehearsals. Verses were sung by a chorus of twenty voices accompanied by an organist and violinist.

When the Vicar opened the pageant in the grounds of the Rectory, he praised all who had worked so hard to make the event possible and mentioned only two people by name. One was D'Arcy de Ferrars and the other was Dorothy Sayers who played the violin and also wrote some of the words. She was the daughter of the Rector of Bluntisham. Later she gained fame as an author writing amongst many other works, the Lord Peter Wimsey novels.

In the October edition of the Parish magazine the accounts showed that £52 was taken at the gate, programmes £3 and refreshments, teas and donations almost £18. After expenses had been deducted the balance was just over £38 which was split three-fifths for the re-roofing of the Parish Church and two-fifths for 'Philanthropic Objects'.

King Henry VIII

Many of the scenes in the pageant were photographed, although in some, characters are blurred presumably because they moved whilst the photograph was being taken. It was thought that copies of some of these photographs had been lost. However, in January 2013 Somersham's Parish Clerk received almost thirty different photographs, some of which were clearly of the pageant with a covering letter from the sender, a man who had been clearing out his deceased mother's possessions. Upon further investigation it became apparent that they were of two separate events, that is, not all were pageant photographs.

Further research in the Church Parish magazines revealed that in 1911, three years after the pageant, Rev. de Courcy-Ireland mindful that the Church's patron saint is John the Baptist, proposed to hold a Mystery Play embodying the events in the life of the saint. D'Arcy de Ferrars once again promised to help.

John the Baptist in Prison (Mystery Play)

Again the performance took place on the Rectory Lawn and was held on 28th and 29th June, the Vicar writing that it "may prove the first mystery play in the open air in modern times". The proceeds were to have been for the Church Restoration Fund but unfortunately the expenses were in excess of the receipts by just over £11, a sizeable amount in those days.

The script of the mystery play was printed in one of the 1911 Parish Magazines and seems to confirm that three of the photographs were of that event.

*Salome (Herod's Daughter) with dancers playing tambourines
(Mystery Play)*

*John Bell has written a book which includes a lot of detail about
the Pageant and some photographs of the event. In Barbara
Hoy's book on Somersham she has included the whole of the
account of the Pageant that appeared on the front page of the
Morning Leader newspaper.*

Hospital Sunday

Up to the outbreak of war in 1939, Somersham's local hospital at
Huntingdon, the old "County Hospital", was maintained chiefly
by private subscription and was respected and revered by all and
sundry. It had a homely feel about it and served a population of
about 40,000. To augment the inflow of cash, towns and
villages alike organised fundraising days which became known
as Hospital Sunday. At Somersham volunteer collectors visited
every home in the Parish, even the most isolated ones scattered
throughout the fens, usually returning with their collecting tins

A float decorated for Hospital Sunday

full to the top. Sunday afternoon was given over to a grand parade of decorated floats, horses, carts, cycles, and a few cars and still more collecting boxes, and headed by the Town Band. The St. Ives Fire Engine always brought up the rear. The event ended on the Cross which by then would be packed with people to witness an open air service and final drumhead collection, usually enthusiastically supported by visiting dignitaries.

SOMERSHAM CELEBRATES ROYAL OCCASIONS

Records show that people in Somersham have celebrated various royal events.

1887 - Golden Jubilee of Queen Victoria - There is a detailed account of the programme of events in Somersham in the Hunts Post dated June 25th, 1887.

The following is an extract from Charles E. Dawes book Somersham Past and Present dated 1890: **1887** — We have no record as to what part Somersham took in the general rejoicings of 1809, at the celebration of George III's Jubilee, but the festivities of 1887 are fresh in the memories of all. The following account of the proceedings is taken from a local paper of June 25th, 1887:— *"The Jubilee of her Majesty Queen Victoria will probably never be effaced from the memory of the inhabitants of Somersham, for it may safely be asserted that hardly ever, if at all, has there been unanimity of purpose to*

equal that exhibited on Tuesday. Long before the general public were astir a merry peal was rung on the Church bells, reminding all of the loyalty it was their duty and privilege to show during the day.

At 11.30 the village band paraded the streets, and thence proceeded to Church, where a service was held at 12.15. The service was fully choral, and the sacred edifice was crowded with members of all denominations and the service was taken part in by the Baptist minister (Rev. J.B. Lamb) who read the lesson. A very appropriate sermon was preached by the Vicar.

On leaving Church the band marched to Mr. Benton's paddock, where 300 persons, including a few ladies, sat down to dinner. After dinner, Mr. Street reminded the company that the day's programme was a long one, and he would therefore only give one toast.

After the toast 'the Queen' had been duly honoured a move was made to Mr. Hinkins' field, where Messrs. Jones, Harris, and Wilson had been, for some days previous, preparing for the sports. These gentlemen were able, with the assistance of the Vicar and the other members of the sports committee (Messrs. F. Watson, W. J. Nicholls, R. Brown, and H. Wiles) to provide sports second to none ever provided in the village.

There were in all 14 races, which, with an interval for tea, lasted till 9.30. The women and children who had tea numbered 615. The bicycle races were finished on the 'Cross' at 9.30 when, with hearty cheers of loyalty, the company separated."

1935 - Golden Jubilee of King George V – The Hunts Post gave details of the *"splendid programme of celebrations carried out in Somersham. Practically every dwelling house and shop* *displayed flags, bunting, coloured paper festoons or symbolic designs and the streets were spanned in many places by gaily decorated streamers."* Over a thousand people attended an open air united service, fancy dress and sports competitions were held and every child received a souvenir mug.

1937 – Coronation of King George VI – There was a programme giving details of a procession and sports on 12th May 1937 and a photograph appeared in the Hunts Post with the caption "Somersham's programme, like most other villages, included a fancy dress parade".

Children in the fancy dress parade
(Coronation of King George VI)

1953 – Coronation of Queen Elizabeth II – A photograph in the Hunts Post (June 4th 1953) with a caption *"Here the people of Somersham begin their day with a service in Church Street".*

The Service in Church Street (Coronation of Queen Elizabeth II)

The open-air united service was followed by the judging of fancy dress groups and then there was a parade headed by Somersham Town Band proceeding through the village to the Norwood Playing Field. Prizes were presented for fancy dress, decorated prams, cycles, cars, lorries, horse drawn vehicles and the best decorated house. Novelty sports races were held on the field and in the evening there was dancing on the lawns at 'The Limes' ending with a torchlight and fancy dress parade.

1977—Silver Jubilee of Queen Elizabeth II - Celebrations followed a similar theme to those of the Coronation but were spread over several days. Things started on Friday with a Jubilee Celebration Dance. The next day there was a Talent Concert in the school. Sunday was marked with church services, a six-a-side cricket match, a concert given by Chatteris Town

Band, Senior Citizens Teas and Community Singing. Monday was a day for the youngsters with a puppet show and tea for those up to age 9 years and in the evening there was a disco for older children. On the Tuesday there was a carnival, that has turned out to be an annual event ever since.

2012 - Diamond Jubilee of Queen Elizabeth II - The village celebrated in a novel way by holding a Royal Garden Party at 'The Limes'. It was organised by the Somersham Garden Club and held in the style of a Victorian event with history, needlecraft and dancing displays, live musical entertainment, periodic loyal toasts, optional period fancy dress and the special appearance of Queen Victoria in the personage of an elderly lady (Pat Spencer) from the village.

BAD TIMES IN THE VILLAGE

In the 18th and 19th centuries Somersham was struck by some terrible events.

The Hurricane

Nathan Dews describes how in September 1741 *"a most extraordinary hurricane from the south-west passed over Somersham. It began exactly at noon and lasted about thirteen minutes, eight of them in full violence. The storm brought with it a mist, and seemingly not thirty yards high from the ground, rolled on at the rate of a mile and a half a minute with a noise like thunder. There are no records to show the damage sustained at Somersham, but at Bluntisham, where the storm was equally violent, the Rectory house was untiled, the statues and balustrades on it down, as also all the stabling, sixty empty barns in the parish, the alehouse; and about twelve dwelling houses out of 100 experienced the same fate; together with all the mills in its track, and many stacks of hay and corn. The birds that were caught in it were dashed to pieces against the ground, and very few trees escaped."*

A Small Pox Epidemic

In his book *"Somersham Past & Present"*, Charles E. Dawes states that in 1759 there was an epidemic of small pox in Somersham and a number of children died from the disease. However, careful examination of the Church Burial Registers shows the first recorded deaths from small pox were in 1765. In fact before that year the cause of death was not given.

There were two deaths from small pox in 1765 and two deaths in each of the years 1766 and 1768 from the disease. In 1769 the burial records show that there were eleven deaths from small pox, three of these being infants.

173

31st March	Mary Sutton	
2nd April	Thomas Sutton	
4th April	Miss Mary Thomson	
5th April	Ann Sutton	Infant
9th April	Mary Topper	
11th April	John Burton	
13th April	Sarah Cook	Infant
16th April	Sarah Westmorland	
28th April	Mary West	Widow
31st May	Susanna Parrot	Infant
21st June	William Glover	

Infant mortality was particularly prevalent in those times. Eighteen of the thirty nine burials in 1769 were infants. The next death from small pox recorded in the registers was in 1784. Periodically other isolated deaths from the disease are recorded.

Cholera Outbreak

In the summer of 1832, there was an outbreak of cholera in the village. Mention is made of this in different books and it is reported as causing the death of 30 people. However, the Church Burial Registers record only 22 persons dying of the disease.

The Rector and the grave diggers must have been very busy as the records below illustrate.

6th June	John Clack	43	Labourer of Warboys
	Thomas Must	42	Shopkeeper
21st June	Joseph Woods	30	Labourer
23rd June	Martha Woods	65	Widow
24th June	George Woods	9	Son of Joseph & Mary
24th June	Richard Woods	18 mths	Son of Joseph & Mary

30th June	Jane Lake	2	Dau. of William & Mary
30th June	Mary Thompson	51	Wife of John
1st July	Richard Cox	6	Son of James & Sarah
3rd July	Sarah Cox	29	
14th July	Samuel Griggs	71	
15th July	William Sneesby	30	
16th July	Thomas Nicholls	26	
16th July	William Sutton	44	
19th July	Sarah Salmons	51	
23rd July	John Sneesby	5	Son of William
23rd July	William Sneesby	2	Son of William
23rd July	Elizabeth Elger	38	Widow
27th July	Mary Corbet	49	
27th July	Thomas Everet	70	
27th July	William Collingwood	60	Wheelwright
6th August	Mary Crow	44	Widow

Fires

Nathan Dews describes how on *"the first of September 1815, a most alarming fire, which at one time threatened the destruction of the whole town, broke out in the centre of Somersham. Every exertion was used to stop the progress of the flames, but all would have been of no avail had not the wind providentially changed. Twenty-four houses, many barns full of corn and several stacks of hay and corn, were at one time all in flames and reduced to heaps of ashes. Property to the amount of £4,000 and upwards was entirely consumed. Few of the thirty-four sufferers from this sad catastrophe saved anything of what they once possessed, and some nothing but the clothes they had on. The fire was accidental, and caused by the firing of Mr. Asplen's copper-chimney. By this severe loss numbers were reduced from a state of comfort to the greatest distress. A meeting of the principal inhabitants was summoned, and it was agreed upon that subscriptions throughout Huntingdonshire and the neighbouring counties should be promoted for the relief of the poor sufferers."*

There were a number of private subscriptions as well as donations from the inhabitants of neighbouring towns and villages in the counties of Huntingdon and Cambridge who sent them to the relief committee at Somersham. The collecting sheets sent in by these places, which contain the names of the subscribers are still preserved.

£151 7s 6d was collected at Somersham, and the Fire Insurance Offices contributed £52 9s. The total amount raised was £1244 15s 7d. An influential committee was appointed to distribute the money raised.

The particulars of the cost of extinguishing the fire, which are inserted in the Parish Registers, contain some interesting matters. The amount spent in bread, cheese, and beer, was £67 3s 9d. Labourers from Chatteris were paid £2 8s 6d, from Pidley £5, from Somersham £26 7s 6d, from Earith £3 8s, from Bluntisham £4 6s, and from Colne 17s. The sum of £5 was paid for *"injuring Mr. Simon's horse in bringing the engine."* The total expense incurred was £156 5s 2d.

At that time the fire engine was kept in the lower part of the Church tower. It was then removed to a position in an engine-house in Church Street near the north-eastern entrance to the churchyard. This building was removed midway through the 20th century.

Further fires in Somersham are reported by Charles Dawes who states that on the 21st March 1855 seventeen families were burnt out and several farm buildings destroyed, although the location of the fire is not given. He then goes on to mention that on Ash Wednesday 1857 a group of four cottages and a public house forming what was known as the 'Red Cow Hill' situated in the centre of the village were totally destroyed by fire. No cause was assigned for either of these fires. The Red Cow public house appears in the 1861 Census, so it would seem that it was either rebuilt or moved elsewhere in the High Street.

The most notorious fire in Somersham occurred on 26th May 1824. Thomas Savage who was 21 years of age was sentenced to death at the Huntingdon Assizes in August 1824 for setting fire to a barn.

The entry in the Church Burial Register for Thomas Savage

The following account of the fire states that *"Savage and two other men named Woods and Cook, arranged to burn down the premises in order that they might steal something. Savage meeting Woods said to him 'I think I shall set fire to old Billy Mason's house - yet I think I shall not - if I set fire to Wellman's or Ibbott's that will spread to Leeds' tithe barn and the two large shops, and then we can make our market; if you stand at my back and hand the old iron chests about we shall never want any more.'*

On the evening of the fire Cook accompanied Savage to the barn, where they remained until one o'clock in the morning, when Savage set fire to the thatch of the barn, Cook looking on. The building was soon in a blaze, and the flames quickly spread to all the buildings between the barn and Mr. Morts' house, which was entirely destroyed.

Cook and Woods afterwards turned King's evidence against Savage, who pleaded guilty, and received sentence of death. "

A certain amount of historical interest is attached to this fire, as Savage was the last person to be executed for incendiarism (arson) in this county. His remains were buried in Somersham churchyard on the 19th December and this is recorded in the Church Burial Register. It is said that his ghost still haunts his former home which now forms part of the Windmill Public House.

Thomas Savage's execution seems excessive compared with present day punishment for crime. However, even crimes that we might regard as petty were punished severely in the 1870s. Typical examples are Charles Duller a 13 year old Somersham boy who was sentenced to seven days hard labour and eight strokes of a birch rod for stealing two rabbits and William Shepherd aged 15 who was given twenty one days hard labour for stealing a coat.

Whilst on the subject of crime, Charles Dawes gives an account of a robbery that took place near Somersham on Saturday, 18th October 1823.

"As John Smith, between sixty and seventy years of age was returning from Cambridge to Somersham by St. Ives afoot, he was met by a strong young fellow, within a mile and a half from home. The young man accosted Mr. Smith with the customary formula used by highwaymen, '*Stand and deliver!*'
'*Deliver what?*' asked Mr. Smith

'*All you have*' said the man, and he instantly wrenched the stick with which Smith was walking from his hand, and struck him a violent blow on the forehead. Smith staggered and fell, and the robber threw himself upon him. '*Do you mean to murder me?*' asked Smith.

'*I mean to have all you have*' replied the robber. Smith then seized fast hold of the highwayman's hair and a fierce scuffle ensued, during which both rose from the ground together. Smith, still retaining hold of his assailant's hair, told him he would have to go back with him. The highwayman refused. '*Then,*' said Smith, '*you shall go forward with me,*' and immediately changing his hold from his hair to his collar he forced him about half-a-mile along the road until they reached a cottage, when Smith called up a man of the name of Savage, who assisted in conveying the highwayman to Somersham, where he was given into the hands of the constables and was afterwards convicted at the Huntingdon Assizes." – Dawes further writes *"The above case is thought not unworthy of public notice. Here is a poor man between 60 and 70 years of age who has displayed all the resolution and firmness of mind which few persons would have done in the zenith of their days. A subscription is begun at Somersham for the above John Smith".*

SOMERSHAM IN THE SECOND WORLD WAR

One of the first impacts that WW2 had on Somersham was the evacuation of children from London in September 1939. Jim Brittain was one of those evacuees and he was housed with the Rowe family at 'The Grange' in the High Street.

Jim and his two brothers missed the initial evacuation, possibly because they were at different schools and their parents wished them to be kept together. Jim was thirteen, Roy was ten and Raymond was seven. In the event they were included in the evacuation that took place on Sunday, 3rd September, 1939 which embraced a large contingent of expectant mothers and school children from North London.

On the train journey they stopped at various stations where they seemed to be unhitching carriages, thus making the train shorter on its journey north. Their carriage was unhitched at Somersham, while the train continued on its way to Chatteris, March and beyond. They left the station and made their way to the centre of the village, about six hundred yards away where they were received in the Village Hall known as the Palace. There they all stood around and Jim held on to his two brothers, as prospective 'fosterers' looked over the evacuees and decided who to take into their households. There was little enthusiasm for taking on a whole family of three boys, and Jim had made it clear that they were to remain as one unit. 'The Palace' was therefore starting to get rather empty, when at last someone decided to take them all. In fact they did not have far to go, for their new home was to be at the Grange in the High Street.

What they did not know was that their foster parents, Mr. Clarence and Mrs. Sarah Rowe, had a family of six children of their own, aged between three and eighteen years old. The

Grange had large cellars, a ground floor, first floor and an attic where they slept. There was an indoor toilet, but no bathroom. Baths were taken in a galvanised bath in the scullery. There were also outside toilets in the garden. Outside there were outbuildings and barns where chickens and a pig were kept, as well as some cows. The land embraced a kitchen garden, lawned garden (including a tennis court) a field and a paddock.

Meals were taken together in the kitchen-dining room around a massive pine farmhouse table, big enough to accommodate the eleven of them. Mrs. Rowe used to serve the vegetables whilst Mr. Rowe carved and served the meat. Leading off the kitchen was a large walk-in pantry. Mrs. Rowe was a very good cook and the kitchen garden ensured a plentiful supply of vegetables and fruit, the latter providing the ingredients for many a tasty pie. Despite the rationing, food was not too much of a problem as there were plenty of vegetables, fruit and eggs. They each had their own allocation of cheese and preserves set aside in the pantry. It was permissible to keep, and kill, one pig for the household and this was, of course, a great help.

As regards school, the village school did not have the necessary spare capacity and all the evacuees were educated in the Wesleyan Chapel in Parkhall Road. This meant that there was only one classroom, with pupils whose ages ranged from five to thirteen years and the older ones were, of necessity left very much to their own devices. Jim had two years French behind him and the local Vicar, Rev. Sheppard gave him some tuition at the Rectory from time to time.

So far as life at the Grange was concerned, the three brothers were accepted fully into the family. Jim subsequently acquired a bicycle and with David Rowe, one of the sons who was about Jim's age, he was able to visit St. Ives, which boasted a cinema,

Chatteris and other villages. In the summer of 1940 he earned some pocket money picking fruit, mainly plums, in orchards around Bluntisham.

Otherwise, spare time was spent in the garden, fields and around the adjoining 'Ballast Hole' lake. During the winter the Rowes lent Jim a pair of 'Fen Runner' ice skates (wooden bodied with inset metal blades) and he joined in the ice skating on the Fen dykes and on the 'Ballast Hole'. The 1940/41 winter was particularly severe and he remembered skating until March, eventually having to jump onto the ice after the edges along the banks had thawed. The ice was extremely thick, possibly fifteen inches, and the fish had died because of the lack of oxygen.

Jim's brother Raymond got bronchitis about six months after being evacuated. He wanted to return home to his mother in London as did the other brother Roy, so they were collected by their parents. Jim wanted to stay in Somersham and the Rowe family were happy to keep him. In April 1941, when Jim was 15, he returned home to get a job.

The Troops
Troops first arrived in Somersham following the Dunkirk evacuation in 1940. They were billeted in various houses throughout the village. More soldiers arrived in time, one group being from the King's Own Scottish Borderers who were billeted in Nissen huts at the Rectory. They marched down the High Street each day at 7.30 am accompanied by bagpipes towards the Palace Hall where they had their canteen. Other large detachments of troops manned anti-aircraft posts and searchlights including a position at North Fen. After D-Day some prisoners of war (POWs) were kept in the village.

Members of the Home Guard from Somersham

The Home Guard

Like most areas of the country units of the Home Guard were set up in Huntingdonshire. It was a defence organisation which was operational from 1940 until 1944 and was made up of local volunteers otherwise ineligible for military service, usually owing to age, hence the nickname 'Dad's Army'. The photograph above shows some of the Somersham men who were members in 1942. Unfortunately one of their number, Leslie Barson, was drowned on a Home Guard exercise at Hemingford Grey. His grave is in Somersham Churchyard.

Air Raid Precautions

The ARP was an organisation dedicated to the protection of civilians from the danger of air-raids. An ARP exercise in Somersham on 19th April 1942 was buzzed by a low-flying RAF aeroplane. The exercise's umpire wrote that it was 'a real test, it gave all personnel an idea of what real blitz conditions would be like, and how difficult first aid work would be when being dive-bombed at the same time.'

Metal Salvage

During the war the need for salvage metal meant iron railings were removed from the front of many buildings across the country, apparently the railings at the Chestnuts (now called the Mulberry House) were spared due to their artistic or historic interest.

The Air Crash

The most traumatic event of the war for Somersham occurred on Monday evening, the 5th October 1942. A Wellington bomber setting off on a raid got into difficulty and lost height and hit some of the chimneys in Saviours Row in Rectory Lane. It then crashed into an 18th century red brick three storey house part of which was at one time the King William IV public house and also demolished the Carpenters Arms, a lath and plaster, beamed and thatched early 17th century beer house. The gap made is now filled by Carpenters Court and a plaque was placed on its wall to mark the event and remember the eleven who died. It was unveiled on the 60th anniversary of the crash.

The Hunts Post reported that the crew of the aircraft had baled out a few minutes before the crash and the plane came down in Somersham's main street. Eleven people, including three generations of the same family, were killed and six houses were wrecked by the crash or gutted in the terrific fire that broke out. The blaze, which was visible for miles, was fought by local firemen, who were said to have done a splendid job and deserved high praise. Members of the Somersham platoon of the Home Guard set to work, soon after the crash, in lending whatever assistance was needed, and they, together with other soldiers and airmen, did heroic work throughout the night and the next day. It was not until after daylight on Tuesday that six of the bodies - burned beyond recognition - were recovered from under the masses of smouldering debris.

The victims of the disaster, which turned the peaceful village street into a scene of devastation were:

Mrs. Violet Moule, 63,
Mrs. Vera Cattenack, 23, her daughter, and
Pauline Cattenack, 1 year, her grand-daughter;
Frank Lamb, 44, labourer, and
Mrs. Alice Lamb, 70, his mother;
Mrs. Elsie May Taylor, 49, and her mother,
Mrs. Annie Holdich, 74;
Mrs. Elizabeth Richardson, 67, an evacuee from Norwich;
Mrs. Eliza Nightingale, 68;
Ena Stroud, 15;
and Juliana Davies.

Newspaper photograph of the crash scene , the broken line indicating the path of the aircraft as it crashed.

The two last-named died in Huntingdon County Hospital. The bodies of the remainder were dug out of the wreckage, those of Mrs. Cattenack and Mrs. Richardson not being recovered until 2.45 pm on Tuesday.

Mrs. Lamb, Mrs. Taylor, Mrs. Holdich, Mrs.Richardson and Mrs Moule were all widows. Mr. and Mrs. John Nightingale, their married daughter, Mrs. Eliza Davies, and the latter's baby, Juliana, were all taken to hospital, where Mrs. Nightingale died later. Mrs. Davies and her daughter had serious burns; but Mr. Nightingale's were not severe. Others rather badly hurt included Mr. S. Turner, who lodged with Mrs. Moule, and Mr. Robert Brown (burned), and Miss Johnson, of Chapel Field (head injury). Ena Stroud, who had recently left school, lived with her parents, who were away moving furniture to a new house when the plane crashed.

What happened, in those few minutes which brought death and destruction to the village were best told in the words of Special Sgt. Norman, who said *"I was sitting indoors about 7.15 pm when I heard a plane 'revving' overhead in a rather peculiar way. I went outside and saw two planes flying around, with a sort of halo round them. I took them to be on fire. Shortly afterwards I saw a plane flying at a great speed in a southerly direction, in a fairly shallow power dive. It came lower and lower and crashed into the houses in West End, which at once went up in a mass of flames."*

Nothing but a few pieces of twisted metal remained of the aircraft on Tuesday morning. The crew who had baled out, landed safely on the Bluntisham to Oldhurst Road, only the pilot sustaining a twisted ankle.

A few days later an inquiry was opened by the County Coroner at Huntingdon County Hospital and evidence of identification was given. The inquest was continued at the Palace, Somersham, where the remainder of the victims were identified.

Flt. Sgt. Peter Trembley, RA.F., said the plane took off about 7 o'clock on Monday evening. He was the rear gunner of a crew of six. "We had been airborne about ten minutes and were flying round to gain height when I heard on the inter-com the front gunner saying he could smell smoke. At that time none of the crew had any idea where the smoke was coming from. A few seconds later it was ascertained that serious trouble had arisen in the aircraft, and the captain, Flt. Sgt. Case, gave the order for all the crew to prepare to bale out. He then gave the order 'Abandon aircraft' and I baled out at 12,000 feet."

When he was descending by parachute he could see that the aircraft that he had abandoned was on fire. When he landed some distance away, he returned to camp. He said that all the crew had baled out safely.

The Coroner returned a verdict of Accidental Death and said that these eleven people died from shock and burns they had received when the houses they lived in were set on fire by this crash. "I find that it was accidental, and express my very sincere sympathy with the relatives in this most unfortunate occurrence. In these days death is ever lurking round the corner for most of us, but it is very sad that a place like Somersham should suffer so bitterly."

The Funeral service and Burials took place on Saturday 10th October and the Hunts Post reported it as follows:

"In the peace of a country churchyard, with strong gusts of wind blowing the autumn leaves across the graves, I watched on Saturday afternoon (writes a "Post" representative) while

Somersham buried its dead. It was a sombre and impressive experience and one that can never be effaced from my memory.

In the presence of the entire village, and of many sympathizers from farther afield, the eleven victims of last week's disaster were borne to their last resting place by men of the Royal Air Force, between motionless ranks of uniformed men and women. The congregation was too large to be accommodated in the church, and the brief simple service took place beside the graves, with the Bishop of Ely offering words of comfort to the bereaved and to the stricken parish as a whole.

What it meant in personal sorrow when the pilotless British aircraft plunged through the thatched cottages in Somersham's main street, killing five widows, two little children, and four others; was shown by the long lines of family mourners which walked behind each gleaming coffin. There were over 200 in the five into which they were divided, and more than 80 followed behind the coffins of Mrs. Violet Moule, her daughter (Mrs. Vera Cattenack) and her grand-daughter, one year-old Pauline Cattenack.

A newspaper photograph of the Funeral Cortege

189

There were ten coffins in all, as Mrs. Cattenack and her baby were buried together. Particularly pathetic was the little one containing the body of four-year-old Juliana Davies, grandchild of Mrs. Eliza Nightingale. Juliana died in Huntingdon County Hospital at 1.30 pm on Wednesday, bringing the death roll up to eleven. Her mother is still detained in the hospital with severe burns.

The coffins were borne to the church on R.A.F. tenders covered with masses of flowers and escorted by a large contingent of airmen. The route from the Chapel Schoolroom was lined by members of the Home Guard and a military unit and the village square was filled with a silent, sorrowing throng.

Parties of R.A.F. men acted as bearers when the church gateway was reached, and here the cortege was met by the clergy – the Bishop of Ely (Dr. H.E. Wynne), the Rev. B. Freer-Shepherd (Rector of Somersham), the Rev. P.F.C. Lamb (Curate), the Rev. J.D. Stewart (former- Rector), and the Rev. E.C. Kearsley Starling (Somersham Baptist minister). The lines of family mourners fell in behind their respective relatives, and each sad procession was preceded by one of the five clergy, declaiming those comforting words "I am the Resurrection and the Life...."

The pathway through the churchyard was lined on one side by blue uniformed men of the National Fire Service and by Red Cross nurses; on the other side by A.R.P. personnel, wearing blue overalls and steel helmets, and by ambulance and first-aid party men. Members of the Somersham platoon of the Home Guard and of the special constabulary formed a square around the graves. Officers of an Army unit and of the Home Guard walked in the cortege and behind them came a slow marching contingent of military.

While the clergy were conducting the short service in the churchyard, a bomber circled overhead and dipped one wing in salute. The Bishop, addressing the immediate mourners, asked them to realise that he came not only to express his own sympathy but also that of the whole diocese of all Cambridgeshire and Huntingdonshire.

"I want you to remember" he went on, "that in this bitter blow which has fallen upon your parish you are very much in the thoughts of many, many people near and far".

Tragically the Wellington X3811 which crashed on Somersham had a crew which included three Canadians, one Australian, and one New Zealander. These men were all killed a few months later in February 1943, together with two R.A.F. flight sergeants who had joined them in flying a Lancaster bomber on a raid on Wilhelmshaven. The names of the seven crew members are commemorated on the Runnymede Memorial as having no known grave.

Somersham Airfields
The most secret events that took place in Somersham during the war concern two fields south to south-west of the village close to the railway track. The first was used from 1941 as the Q site for RAF Wyton and was a phoney airfield; the sites were named after the decoy 'Q' vessels used during the First World War. They were designed to confuse the Germans and hopefully draw air attacks away from proper operational airfields. Some Q sites had dummy hangars, living quarters and even mock aircraft to make the sites look realistic from aerial photographs, but this probably wasn't the case in Somersham. It would seem that the airfield was never attacked and towards the end of 1942, like most other Q sites, it was closed down.

However, from the autumn of 1942 another airfield closer to Cuckoo Bridge was used by Lysanders and Hudsons of 138 and 161 Squadrons at RAF Tempsford, which were engaged on secret operations. The fact that it was in a secluded position not visible from any road and hidden over the brow of the hill from the village made it ideal to practise night-landings and take-offs, that would be used in the deployment and collection of secret agents in pitch black conditions. Remarkably it is the same shape and size today. Residents at the time saw the planes approaching and taking off, but could not see what was happening on the ground.

The RAF collaborated with SIS (Special Intelligence Service commonly known as MI6) in arranging to land and pick up agents and material from France in light aircraft. Agents and pilots alike took great personal risk during these operations. Pilots had to navigate by map, timing and sight, find and land in fields in the dead of night. Agents had to slip away into the countryside, constantly aware that the enemy could discover them at any moment. They were the bravest of the brave. Landings were made in the Unoccupied Zone ("Vichy France") until that too was occupied. Agents who preferred not to parachute out could be landed, not only with radios, weapons and other military material, but also with useful stuff for winning friends, such as chocolate, tobacco and real coffee. Obviously more agents came in than out in this manner (though a few got away by sea), material coming in included maps and plans of German installations, information on troop movements, and luxuries such as cognac, champagne and perfume.

Each operation had to be organised by an 'Operator', usually a Frenchman who had come into Britain. They were given their training at RAF Tempsford for a few weeks before being landed or parachuted back to France. The agents and instructors were billeted in Farm Hall, Godmanchester whilst they were being trained. The agents were driven over to Somersham for practical sessions dressed as Army Officers. Air Raid Wardens in Somersham were instructed never to stop black curtained cars that swept in and out of the village in the small hours of the morning.

Operators were also trained in choosing suitable fields, making sure there were no hidden ditches and no tall trees or other obstacles too close to the chosen area. They practised all over Huntingdonshire, also measuring the fields and encoding the descriptions ready to do this on their return to France so that they could make radio transmissions back to England.

The field at Somersham was ideal for pilots and agents to use for practice in both the daytime and at night. Daylight practice was done with square boards attached to poles to indicate the position for the lights: at night, and for real operations, these were ordinary hand-held torches. They were laid out in the form of an inverted L, two lights (A and B) were in a straight line about 150 metres apart, and the third (C) was about 50 metres off to the right of B. The pilots would attempt to touch down to the right of A, run along between B and C, turn to the right around C and return to the right of A. The Operator and outgoing agents would be waiting to the left. The Operator would get his passengers and all baggage out of the plane, then load more baggage and passengers and take off again into the wind, ideally not more than five minutes after landing.

Although the squadron was based at RAF Tempsford, actual operations were normally flown from RAF Tangmere, south of Chichester.

The best description of the whole business is in Hugh Verity's book 'We Landed by Moonlight', which reveals that exactly the same procedure, with the same aircraft and pilots, was used by SOE (Special Operations Executive), indeed on some occasions people from both organisations came in together but the two organisations loathed each other. SOE went public soon after the war, whilst SIS still keeps very quiet.

Doodle Bug Explosion
A real danger still existed from 1944 onwards in the form of German V1 weapons (doodle bugs) aimed at London but occasionally crashing off course. On 18th March 1945 a V1 landed and exploded along the footpath between Church Street and Colne damaging one hundred and ninety properties, including one hundred and eighty three domestic houses (mainly broken windows).

The War Memorial
After the War the Parish Council discussed the idea of having a memorial to the Somersham men who had lost their lives serving

The names on the War Memorial:

Peter S. Barlow
Leslie J. Barson
Reginald H. Behagg
Alfred Bell
William Butler
Douglas W. Dew
Douglas K. Lowe
Frederick C. Seamark
Stanley Smith
Robert W. Thomas
Sidney A. Thomas
John West
Dennis E. Whitfield

Members of the British Legion take the salute

their country, but it was not until 1957 that the granite stone at the Cross in the centre of the village was erected. The following account is adapted from a report in the Hunts Post dated 21st November 1957.

Somersham's Memorial to the thirteen men of the village who fell in the 1939 – 1945 war was unveiled by Wing-Cmdr. A.M. Brown of RAF Wyton, on Sunday 17th November 1957. It was dedicated by the Rector of Somersham, the Rev. G.W. Coupe.

Crowds of people lined the village streets to watch a parade to the memorial which was headed by Somersham Town Band. Eleven British Legion standards were carried in the parade, including two county standards.

Rev. Coupe conducted the service, assisted by the Rev. R.J. Stephens (Baptist Minister) and the church choir led the singing of "All people that on earth do dwell". Prayers led by Rev. Coupe were followed by the unveiling and Wing-Cmdr. Brown's address. He said the ceremony was an important and solemn one for Somersham. It was fitting that the names of those who sacrificed their lives should be recorded in stone, and fitting that people today should show their gratitude in singing hymns and in prayers.

The RAF Band take the salute as they march past the War Memorial

The hymn "O God our help" was sung, and wreaths were laid by representatives of the various organisations in Somersham as well as by relatives of the fallen. The Town Band played for the singing of the National Anthem, and after the Benediction, Wing-Cmdr. Brown took the salute at a march past. He said it was an honour for a representative of RAF Wyton to be asked to unveil the memorial and appropriate that the Royal Air Force should represent the Services at the unveiling for it was from this area that the Pathfinder Force and the bomber streams set off to battle and lost so many men.

The roll of honour and the Legion's exhortation were read by Mr. Cherrington (Clerk to the Parish Council) and the Last Post was sounded by an RAF Sgt. Bugler.

SPORT AND SPORTS CLUBS

Cricket

The first recorded instance of a cricket club in the village was in the May 1875 Church Parish Magazine when it was reported that a meeting had been held to form a Somersham United Cricket Club. The newly formed club covered Bluntisham, Colne, Earith, Fenton and Pidley as well as Somersham. The first match was played on the 20th May between the married and the unmarried members. They played on the field in front of the Rectory, opening on to the Pidley Road, commonly known as 'Newlands' field. It is not known how long the club lasted but by 1907 several of the other villages had their own teams. There was then a Somersham Cricket Club, which opened a pavilion paid for with money donated by prominent men in the village. Their fixture list in 1907 had twenty matches. In 1924 the club could not find a field on which to play their home matches, although several away matches were played, and the club seems to have disbanded.

In 1936 a public meeting was held in the school room to make an effort to re-form the club although they still lacked a suitable field. Later that year they had the offer of a field that they then rented for five years. It was also decided that the club should be called Somersham Town Cricket Club.

It seems that the club then disbanded again, presumably because of the war and may not have reformed until April 1954. The club then played on the Norwood Field and the changing facilities were an old tin hut on the site of the current Victory Hall.

The club really took off in the 1970s when it was reformed and entered the Cambridge Cricket Association League (CCA), playing in the Junior League structure. They also entered the

Somersham Town Cricket Team in 1978
Winners of Junior League Division 4 North

newly formed Fenland League which plays on Sundays and incorporates clubs from the fen land area.

Over the years many league titles have been won by the 1st and 2nd teams as they started from the bottom in Division 7 North and worked their way up to the highest echelons of the Junior League.

In 2007 the club moved to the new Millennium Field facility which is the envy of many visiting teams. 2009 saw the club's greatest achievement when the 1st Xl won the Junior League Div 1 North title and were promoted into the CCA Senior League.

Somersham Town Football Club was formed in 1893 and the

club has played in local league football for many years. It was not until after the Second World War that the club began to emerge as a force in local football. In 1949 they were one of the founder members of the Peterborough and District Premier Division, and for almost forty years were stalwarts of that league finishing runners-up on a number of occasions, but never actually winning the Championship.

Hunts Junior League Champions 1934-35

However, the club was beginning to progress off the field, and in 1981 it purchased their present West End premises and opened their clubhouse.

On the field a significant move was made in the 1988/89 season when the club left the Peterborough League to become founder members of Division One of the Jewson League, in which it remained until 2003/04. On 11th March 1991 the inaugural match under floodlights was played - a Hinchingbrooke Cup match with Potton United, which the visitors won 5-3 after extra time. Later that year a crowd of 537 witnessed the formal opening of the lights when a multi-talented Norwich City side including several international players visited Somersham for a friendly match.

Recent highlights include winning the Hunts Senior Cup in 1993/94, and 2000/01. Other honours include winning the Hinchingbrooke Cup in 1953/54, and the Hunts Junior Cup on three occasions. 2012 also saw the clubs reserve side bring silverware to the club, by winning the Lower Junior Cup.

Somersham had a ladies football team in the late 1940s.

Somersham Town Bowls Club was formed in 1920. It was a strictly private club open to privileged business men, farmers and ministers of the church and chapel.

The founder was Mr. W.H. Gotobed, the senior resident, butcher, farmer and Chapel Deacon, who supplied the bowling green which was adjacent to his property (the Chestnuts) at the rear of the Rose and Crown public house and bounded by the north side of the Wesleyan Methodist Chapel.

The year 1930 saw a change in the club's attitude to membership qualifications, new members were being encouraged and a proposal was put forward by a member that a women's section be formed for afternoon play, but this idea was rejected.

In 1957 the club supported the newly formed Huntingdonshire Bowling Association which is affiliated into county championships. The following year E.W. Moule and H. Bitten won the pairs and then went on to win the National Title at Skegness.

Somersham Bowls Club Ladies team that were winners of Huntingdonshire Ladies League 2012

The 1961 AGM revived the proposal of a women's section, for pressure from some members had been mounting during the season. In fact some women had been invited to the green for practise at times when the members opposing were away and this caused quite a stir in the club.

The point had been made and when put to the meeting the vote was unanimous in favour of a women's section to be formed and this has proved to be one of the soundest decisions the club has made.

The formation of the women's section coincided with the formation of Huntingdonshire Women's Bowling Association and its affiliation to the EWBF (English Women's Bowling Federation). It can be noted that Somersham women won the pairs and two wood triples in their first year of bowling.

In 1964 the club's secretary was notified that the ground on which the green was laid had been sold for development and they would have to abandon it at the end of the season. However, in March that year the chairman notified members that land was available for laying a full-sized green. The site belonged to two members who were prepared to let the club develop it. This was a daunting task as it was a sloping orchard and fruit land. Thanks to the combined efforts of many of the members led by Bill Rickwood, the green was laid and a pavilion erected twelve months later in 1965.

The club has continued to progress: a licensed bar, tool sheds, outside toilets and car park have been added. During the 1973/4 winter an enlarged pavilion including new dressing rooms, kitchen and toilets was made possible by the voluntary help of members.

Quoits is a traditional game which involves throwing metal rings a set distance to land over or near a spike called a hob. It was a game that enjoyed popularity in the village in Victorian times and probably continued well into the 20th century with it being played at the back of some public houses. The photograph opposite is of an original poster advertising a game which shows that there was a Somersham Quoits Club.

Other Sports At various times in the last century there have been hockey, tennis and netball teams and darts was popular in some public houses. The present main participation sports are squash (the Parish Council has a court in the Norwood Building)

badminton, indoor archery and judo whilst activities like Pilates and Ladies Keep Fit also take place in the Victory Hall.

OTHER VILLAGE ORGANISATIONS

Somersham has a very active community life with many organisations meeting in various venues. One only has to look in 'Somersham 4U' (Parish Council Magazine) to get a flavour of what is happening. I have chosen to write about a few of some of the longest established organisations.

Somersham Town Band

There was a time when there were ten or more brass bands in Huntingdonshire but now Somersham Town Band is probably the only genuine one left. Somersham has boasted a band since 1850 but the Somersham Town Band was not formed until 1918 just after the First World War; when their instruments cost £112 as compared to today's £60,000!

Somersham Town Band (Pre-War)

In 1940 it was disbanded and the uniforms, instruments and equipment were held in trust by the Parish Council. Those members remaining in the village were allowed to keep their uniforms but those leaving to join the forces had to hand theirs in. Later that year the band was re-organised and their property was released on condition that if the band dissolved at any time it had to be returned to the care of the council.

The Band was entering contests as early as the 1950s, but unfortunately by 1962 the increasing competition of television had led to it being broken up again. However in 1980 David Chambers, the current Musical Director, was persuaded by some young players from the local primary school, to reform the Band and it has gone from strength to strength ever since.

The re-formed Somersham Town Band

Somersham Town Band is a totally independent organisation with charity status relying on donations, subscriptions and the hard work of its members to say nothing of the support and generosity of Somersham residents.

The Band has a full programme of engagements throughout the year, particularly during the Summer and Christmas periods, with a series of concerts and engagements that cover a wide variety of music, which includes not only traditional marches, but also light classics, medleys of music by famous composers, film and TV themes.

In 1992 the band toured Germany playing at a number of venues. The current band celebrated its 25th anniversary in 2005.

Somersham Town Band also has an active training band for junior members most of whom pass through the main band before going on to further education. It is perhaps a testimony to the quality of this training that several previous members of the band are now playing at professional level in bands and orchestras throughout the country.

The Royal British Legion
A Somersham Branch of the British Legion was formed in 1921, the same year that the national body was set up as an organisation for ex-servicemen and women. The Legion was granted a Royal Charter on 29th May 1971 to mark its fiftieth anniversary which gives the Legion the privilege of the prefix 'Royal'.

In January 1957 it was decided to start a Women's Section within the Somersham Branch. The members raised funds to buy a standard and this was dedicated on 16th June that year in a service held in the Church with over one hundred people in attendance. The event started with a parade from the Palace to the Church headed by Somersham Town Band, which was augmented by bandsman from RAF Oakington. There were eleven standards in the parade and the British Legion County Chairman took the salute.

Like all Royal British Legion Branches Somersham has a branch standard which is paraded on special occasions, most importantly at the annual Act of Remembrance at the War Memorial at the Cross. The current standard was dedicated in the Parish Church on Sunday 18th May 1969.

The Hunts Post records that it was a memorable day for the

members of the Somersham and District British Legion as after many years of service their old standard was handed over for safe keeping and a new standard dedicated. The ceremony was conducted by the Rector (The Rev. T.W. Jones) who received the old standard in the presence of a large congregation. The branch was supported by representatives of other branches in the county. Twenty-eight standards made a colourful and impressive sight as the parade marched behind the Band of RAF Wyton.

Dedication of the new British Legion standard in 1969

Dedication of the Women's Section standard in 1957

As the ceremony began the old standard was taken to the altar by the Rector, and the new standard was unfurled and dedicated. The lines "To the Fallen" were read and the Last Post and Reveille were sounded by a bandsman. After the service the salute at a march past of the two hundred on parade was taken at the Cross by Group Captain Rake. Later members of the Women's Section served refreshments in the Palace to nearly three hundred visitors.

The Royal British Legion uses a hall, situated in the High Street next to 'The Limes'. It was formerly known as the 'Palace'. It is said to have been an old mission hut from the East End of London which was brought up to Somersham by Bernard (Bernie) Criswell. He used it as a weekly cinema and also for dances and darts matches. During the Second World War the Palace was requisitioned by the army and served as their canteen. Bernie sold the Palace to his brother Joe after the war, who in 1948 passed it to a group of men who acted as trustees and allowed the Somersham Branch of the British Legion to use and occupy the building for their activities.

Since that time the building has undergone a number of changes. The Legion converted the central hall into a social club in order to provide a comfortable meeting place for members to socialise in a convivial atmosphere without fear of unruly behaviour or offensive language. It was officially opened by Hugh Linford (President) on Friday 18th July 2003. Other parts of the building have been let out to the Centurion Club and a takeaway food outlet.

The Women's Institute
Somersham branch of this national organisation was formed in 1936 with forty eight members. At the first meeting members agreed to acquire a 'maternity bag' for use at village homebirths. During the Second World War members collected and donated

Somersham Women's Institute Choir in 1953

eggs to Huntingdon Hospital, socks were knitted for servicemen, ladies recruited for the land army, evacuees were cared for and a new canning machine was purchased. Kneelers have been made for the parish church, blankets knitted for Hinchingbrooke Hospital, quilts made to be raffled or donated and a beautiful patchwork tablecloth was made for use at meetings. During the 1980s a WI Dance Group (the Strollers) was very active and not only entertained other members but also other organisations and residents of the local retirement complex. In the 1990s the WI was able to donate some specialist equipment to the local doctor's surgery, which later helped to save a patient's life in an emergency situation.

Its meetings are held monthly with visiting speakers talking about a wide variety of subjects. There are outings to shows and places of interest, initially made by train when there was a station in the village, but now members use the local coach firm.

In 1986 for the Institute's 50th birthday a sub-committee was formed to create a WI Golden Jubilee Book that represented the life of the WI and the village. This happened again for the 75th anniversary in 2011. Both books are kept at Huntingdonshire Archives and can be viewed there.

The WI is an integral part of the community and over the years has been very involved with various projects. In 1945 a member was elected to serve on the St. Ives Rural Housing Committee and participated in plans to build council houses locally. At one time two members represented the WI on the Playing Field Entertainment Committee, while the branch has also made suggestions for facilities in the village that have been implemented by the Parish Council. The Meals on Wheels Service started in the village in 1969 and members raised money to support this plus helped with the deliveries.

The Mothers' Union
A preliminary meeting regarding the formation of the Mothers' Union was held on the 4th March 1912 when Mrs John Clay of Cambridge explained the aims and objects of the Union. The rules at the time stated that three months should elapse before a branch could be started. The Somersham branch was therefore formed on 26th July 1912 when sixteen members and four associates were admitted at a special service. It is interesting to note the difference between a member and an associate. The former was a "married women in all ranks of life" and the latter was "an unmarried women who had charge of, or an interest in, children". Meetings appear to have been held monthly from that time.

The Mothers' Union banner appears to have been purchased in 1932 after events had been held to raise money to buy it. A Parish Magazine from that year reports that only a further £1 12s 9d was needed to pay for the banner. There is a report of the banner being taken to a Deanery Festival at Ramsey on 15th June 1932 where *"it was greatly admired"*. However, I have been unable to find out when it was actually dedicated. The banner is still on display in the Church.

In May 1935 over three hundred members were present at the Deanery of St. Ives Festival. The large company assembled on the Cross and with their branch banners proceeded to the Parish Church. *(Photograph above)*

Somersham Carnival
In 1977 it was the Queen's Silver Jubilee and a group of business owners decided to re-create the pageants from the turn of the century and agreed that the celebrations in Somersham would take the form of a carnival. This started what has now become an annual event.

The May Queen of 1977 was asked to be the Carnival Princess and with her attendants lead a procession in a horse drawn carriage followed by a parade of floats from the pre-school, school and local businesses to the Norwood Field where stalls and teas were to be enjoyed by all. Carnival Week included cricket matches, a children's tea party and a talent show.

A float in the 1977 Somersham Carnival

At the AGM each September the retiring committee along with interested volunteers elect a new committee (usually consisting in the main of the previous year's committee) and great ideas for the next year are discussed and a new theme chosen. Those attending have a genuine desire to bring the local community together at Carnival time and take forward new ideas for activities alongside the traditional favourites. The event owes its success to its independence, creativity and self-funding. Profits are ploughed back into community groups, who apply for grants each year to fund projects that they wish to pursue. Local businesses, organisations and individuals provide support through advertising in the programme, donating raffle prizes and services such as marquees, skips, transport, floats, and signage for free or at reduced rates.

Christmas Lights
Although not an organisation as such, it is well worth mentioning a band of people whose work is much appreciated every year at Christmastime. A working party of volunteers start

putting up the lights in November and raffle tickets are sold for a grand draw.

On the 1st December every year the switch-on takes place. Part of the High Street is closed to traffic and large numbers of villagers and their children pack into the area around 'The Cross', the Junior Town Band play carols, the draw prizes are displayed, mince pies, shortbread and mulled wine are dispensed. At 7 pm the lights are switched on by children from the village schools, Father Christmas arrives in his sleigh, giving sweets to the children and the grand draw takes place.

Youth Organisations
The village also has had various youth movements over the years. The Boys' Brigade and the Girls' Brigade were active organisations in Somersham in the past and there are still Scout and Guide groups in existence at the present time.

INTERESTING FINDS

Over the years some interesting finds have been made in the parish. Nathan Dews in his book 'History of Somersham' writes that about 1731, near the Chatteris Road leading out of Somersham, in a piece of fen land, a plough turned up and broke a small urn containing a few Roman coins. Soon afterwards nearby, another urn which contained about sixty coins, mostly copper, of the later Roman Emperors was found. In 1824, about two miles from Chatteris, another earthen vessel was ploughed up. It contained about a thousand copper coins, chiefly of the Emperors Constantius and Constantine who ruled between A.D 305 and 307. Whilst the railway was being constructed in 1847 an interesting Roman relic that consisted of a small sacrificial cup made of bronze, about 15cm in height was discovered in the cutting between St. Ives and Somersham. Of lesser significance the old OS maps show that a skull was discovered in 1883 north of Rectory Lane.

However, it is still possible to make interesting discoveries. In 2011 a small brass button was found by a lady digging in her garden in the High Street. The inscription on the button is:

GEO.ELMER SOMERSHAM

The 1851 Census for Somersham shows that there was an Elmer family living in the High Street. Head of household was Richard Elmer aged 48 who was a tailor, his wife Elizabeth 38, and two sons George aged 11 who was an apprentice tailor and Lewis aged 10 a scholar. In the 1861 census George Elmer, son of Richard is also recorded as a tailor, now 21 years old.

In Kelly's Directory 1864 - George Elmer is recorded as a tailor (but there is no Richard Elmer), while in Harrod's Directory 1876 George is recorded as a tailor and woollen draper in Somersham.

George obviously had custom made buttons produced to sew on the garments that he sold.

People sometimes dig up bottles in their gardens. An interesting find can be an old bottle with a marble in the neck and a constriction that keeps it in place. These are known as Codd bottles, after their British inventor Hiram Codd who realised that he could seal fizzy drinks in a bottle without using a stopper by putting a marble in the neck of the bottle. The pressure of the drink forces the marble against the upper ring of the neck making a very good seal.

Many of these old bottles have the following moulded in the glass "J GOODENOUGH SOMERSHAM" on one side and on the other "CODD'S PATENT GROOVE" and "MAKERS SYKES MCVAY & THE CODD BOTTLE Co. Ld." In Somersham Joshua Goodenough, the village chemist, was a manufacturer of aerated water and obviously had custom made Codd bottles produced to sell his product.

On 6th August 2009 a bottle was found at Bellevue (15 High Street) when building work was being carried out in the house. The bottle had a piece of paper in the neck which was carefully

This is a photograph of the piece of paper

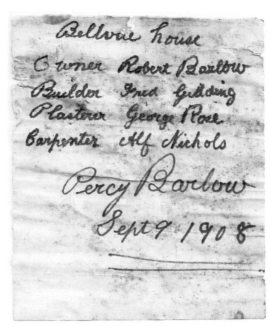

extracted with some tweezers.

The Church baptism records show that there was a Percival Robert Barlow born in 1892 who was almost certainly the Percy Barlow who wrote the note in the bottle. His father was Robert Barlow (owner) who has various entries in Kelly's Directories

Kelly's Directory Entries for Robert Barlow
1898 Rate Collector
1906 Gravel Merchant, Fruit grower and collector of the King's taxes
1910 Fruit grower and collector of the King's taxes
1914 Fruit grower and collector of the King's taxes
1936 Offal Merchants (Bellevue, High Street)
He did not appear in the 1940 edition.

Robert Barlow is buried in Somersham Parish Churchyard, he died on 13th September 1937 aged 75. I have not been able to

219

find any further information about Percy Barlow.

Who knows what other interesting finds will be discovered in the future.

RECENT VILLAGE HISTORY

History is all about recording the events of the past. What may have happened yesterday, last week, last year are often worth recording and so in this final chapter I have picked out a few items that I think are significant, although I have touched upon others earlier in the book.

The Millennium

Six enthusiastic people in the village formed a committee and fulfilled three essential aims over a twenty six month period. Firstly they provided Somersham with a 'Millennium Night to

Remember' consisting of a New Year's Eve dance, followed by a candlelight procession to The Cross, where an estimated two thousand people had assembled to revel in the new millennium. A large video screen backdrop mounted to the rear of a stage supported local entertainers, and a firework display completed the evening. Some villagers saying that it was the "Biggest event in Somersham since VE Day".

Secondly, a carved pictorial sign was commissioned and erected in co-operation with the Somersham Carnival Committee. The Town's people selected the final design from a competition. (See chapter on Village Features).

Thirdly, The Somersham Millennium Stone was sited as a permanent memorial to the year 2000. It was unveiled on 26th

May 2001 and marks the existence of the Greenwich Zero Meridian that uniquely passes through the town and it has a time capsule buried beneath it.

Hattie's Map of Somersham

In August 2012 David Bonnett unveiled the historic map of Somersham branded affectionately by the working group as 'Hattie's map'. The map incorporates the village as it is today together with the old names and places plus photographs. Hattie Skeggs had been helping a working party from the Parish Council to put the map together using her in-depth knowledge of Somersham and its historic names. Sadly she died before it was completed.

Hattie had lived her entire life in Somersham and served the local community as a District and a Parish Councillor as well as being actively involved in many aspects of village life.

The Library

A mobile library used to visit the village every Friday and alternate Tuesdays for many years. Then in 1990 the County Council promised that Somersham would get a library in that financial year. It opened in the first week of July 1991 and Norma Major performed the opening ceremony on 26th September. However, in December 2002 the County Council announced that a quarter of Cambridgeshire's libraries could close. Early in 2003 it was confirmed that the library in Somersham would be one of them, but there were considerable protests from villagers who formed a group called 'Friends of Somersham Library', soon to be known by its acronym FOSL. Just one week after it was closed the library was re-opened by FOSL as a Community Information Centre run by a team of over fifty volunteers and supported by the County and Parish Councils. The building was refurbished and provided with three computers and a thousand books, other books were donated making it over four thousand books. The centre offered photocopying and fax facilities for customers and it opened for four hours more than the former library.

In 2007 the Community Information Centre was awarded the Queen's Award for Volunteers. Julie Liddle (FOSL Chairman at the time) told the local press that the irony was that the County Library Services are very proud of the service that we provide. The award was presented by the Lord Lieutenant of Cambridgeshire in July that year and six members of FOSL attended Buckingham Palace garden parties that summer.

Somersham Goes 'Green'
In 2008 the Parish Council adopted an environmental policy that led to Somersham being the first village in Huntingdonshire to become free of plastic bags. Shops and businesses in the village agreed to co-operate with this initiative which led to every household being given a free re-usable cotton bag for their shopping. The bags can still be bought for £1 but some shops are now issuing plastic bags to their customers if they want one.

Villagers protest against Tesco Express
Early in 2011 villagers were shocked to learn that the Black Bull public house had closed and been sold to the supermarket chain

Tesco. Many people feared that a Tesco Express in Somersham could threaten the viability of the existing shops and that if those shops closed it would affect the vibrancy of the village. One Saturday about one hundred and fifty people staged a protest waving placards and chanting 'Tesco out'. The Parish Council held an open forum at the start of one of their meetings in order to let villagers express their concerns. The shop does not seem to have had a noticeable effect on the village, although it would appear that a lot of people either boycott the shop or at least make sure that they support the 'One-Stop' shop that houses the post office in case that should close and the village lose an important amenity.

PRESERVING SOMERSHAM'S HERITAGE

I mentioned earlier in the chapter about the Church the booklet 'A Brief History of St John the Baptist Church, Somersham' written by the Rev. Coupe, who was Somersham Rector from 1955 – 1959. In the Church Parish Magazine of June 1958 he wrote the following:

"While writing the short history of Somersham Church, it occurred to me time and again how fascinating it would be to be able to see a picture of the village as it was, say, in 1250 or even in 1850. But one can only guess. Through the centuries our villages are always changing, as old houses fall into disrepair and new ones are built, and as our manner of life changes. We cannot now do anything about the distant past, but we can do something about the recent past. Some of you probably possess old photographs, newspaper cuttings, etc., which illustrate the appearance of the villages, the types of vehicles and farm machinery used, the fashions of dress during the past fifty years. In time to come these will be of very great value to all who are interested in the history of the villages, and it is a great shame that they should just be thrown away and lost, as so often happens. In all three churches there is a parish chest where such things could be safely stored, and would be available to all who are interested in them, now and in the future. I would, therefore, appeal to all who possess such pictures and documents, either to let me deposit them in the parish chests now, or if you wish to retain them during your lifetime, to bequeath them to your parish church. They may not seem important to you but you will gain the gratitude of posterity by seeing they do not get lost."

I guess that his words fell on deaf ears as I do not know of any such material in the parish chests, certainly not in the one that is in St John's in Somersham. However, he may, or may not, have inspired Cecil Grimwood (a local builder) to collect many artefacts and memorabilia connected with the village which he displayed as a museum close to his house. Unfortunately I never saw his collection as I came to the village after he and his wife had died and the museum pieces had been dispersed. I have heard about them from many people and no one seems to know precisely what happened to the collection. It is said that an advertisement was posted in the window of one of the shops inviting people who had donated items to collect them and that the remainder of the collection went to an auction house. It seems that many items of Somersham's heritage were lost. The Parish Council had hoped to find a permanent home for the museum collection.

In my research for the Heritage Exhibitions and for this book I have collected together a great deal of information and photographs. Most of the photographs I have borrowed and scanned so the collection is stored digitally on my computer. This book represents a sizable amount of the information that has been amassed. The photographs that I have included are but a fraction of the three hundred or so that I have scanned. I hope that what I have put together supplements and compliments what other local authors have done in the past and every effort has been made to check that the information included is accurate. Perhaps other people will continue to collect together information about the village as it develops in the future.

Appendix A: The Listed Buildings

1 & 3 Church Street
2 & 4 Church Street
5 Church Street
6 Church Street
18 Church Street
21 & 23 Church Street
Bridge to Park Farm
Park Farmhouse, Church Street
Park Farm Cottage, Church Street
Stables in the North West Corner of Park Farmyard
Boundary Wall, Church Street
Church of St John the Baptist
20 & 22 High Street
34 High Street
36 High Street
38 High Street
44 High Street
50 High Street
57 High Street
58 High Street
59 & 61 High Street
60, 62 & 64 High Street
The Grange, 65 High Street
Barn to the rear of 65 High Street (The Grange)
Wisteria House, 69 High Street
Baptist Church, High Street
Braunston House, 72 High Street
Tollington House, 78 High Street
93 High Street
95 High Street
Dovecote in the Church Burial Ground
Tithe Barn adjacent to 96, High Street

97A & 97B High Street

Rose & Crown Public House

100 High Street

101 High Street

103 High Street

The Chestnuts, 105 High Street (now renamed 'The Mulberry House) and Boundary Wall attached to West running North, and short section returning to East

111 High Street

Stable & Coach House to 117 High Street

125 High Street

21 & 23 Parkhall Road (Manor Hall)

Wesleyan Chapel, Parkhall Road

The Rectory, Rectory Lane

Telephone Kiosk, The Cross

Milestone to the South West of the Crollodes Farmhouse

Milestone adjoining 19, The Bank, Chatteris Road

Milestone, North of Mayfield, Chatteris Road

Milestone adjacent to the Hollow, St. Ives Road

Milestone, North East of Cuckoo Bridge Cottage, St. Ives Road

Milestone South East of Rectory Farm, Pidley.

Appendix B: Former Somersham Shops

The following list gives the names of some of the shops that used to be in Somersham over many years.

Name	Business	No.	Street
A Skeggs & Son	Butcher	1	Church St.
J Wakefield	Barber	1	Church St.
Saint Bros.	Family Butchers		Feoffees Rd.
Harry Lane	Grocer	27	High Street
Bert. Corney	Hairdresser	42	High Street
E.W.Moore	Shoe Shop	50	High Street
Eva's	Wool, Baby linen, Lingerie, Knitwear	54	High Street
Margaret M Brownsey	Ladies & Children's Wear etc	54	High Street
R T Senescall	Pet Shop	54	High Street
Ver-Dor	Haberdashery	54	High Street
J Linford	Butcher	56	High Street
W.H.Gotobed	Butcher	56	High Street
Able Ison	Sweet Shop	63	High Street
May Elmore	Sweet Shop	63	High Street
Jack Saint	Baker	66	High Street
Myrtle Aubrey	Hairdresser	66	High Street
S J H Shadbolt	General Stores	73	High Street
Gordon Casburn	Tea Shop/ Cafe	75	High Street
Campbell Flowers	Florist	85	High Street
Elizabeth	Unisex Hair Stylist	87	High Street
Ollie Gibson	Shoe Repairs	91	High Street
Walter Aubrey	Greengrocer	93	High Street
Chas. Norman	Drapery & Clothing	97	High Street

B. Haynes	Grocer & Newsagent	103	High Street
Bonnetts	Bakers	105	High Street
Décor & Handicrafts	Decorating & D.I.Y.	113	High Street
Walter Summers	Baker, Confectioner & General Stores	115	High Street
C A Bull	Baker & Confectioner		High Street
C E Page	Butcher		High Street
C Saint	Baker & Grocer		High Street
Cauldron	Grocer		High Street
Cooper	Hairdresser		High Street
Ernest Smith	Grocer		High Street
Farrow	Wet Fish		High Street
Frank Allen	Undertaker		High Street
Fred Parsons	Butcher		High Street
G Lewis	Baker & Confectioner		High Street
George Grimwood	Grocery Hardware		High Street
Goldsby	Clocksmith		High Street
H J Curry	Hairdressing Saloon		High Street
H. Barlow	Saddler & Leather		High Street
Metcalfe	Coal Merchant		High Street
R Brown & Son	Basket Manufacturer Osier Grower		High Street
Rand	Butchers		High Street
Tom Grounds	Painter & Decorator		High Street
W J Norman	Watch & Clockmaker		High Street
Walter Webb	Grocery & Provisions		High Street
Whitehouse	Grocer		High Street
Reg. Manley	Fish Shop	5	Parkhall Rd.
George Lewis	Bookmaker	11	Parkhall Rd.
Alf Cox	Shoe Repairs		Rectory Lane
C.R. Grimwood	Builder/Decorator		Rectory Lane

Name	Trade	Location
John Saint	Butcher	Rectory Lane
Stanley Brooks	Grocer	Rectory Lane
F Garrood	General Stores	The Bank
W.R. Luck	General Stores	The Bank
Whitehead	Bank Stores 'The Handy Shop'	The Bank
H Hurst	Newsagent etc.	The Cross
A.W. & D.M. Turner	Fish & Chip Shop	West End
C Hazel	Boot & Shoe Repairer	West End
Fred Joyce	Basket Maker	West End
Richard Brown	Baker	
Whitworth's Stores		

INDEX

This is not a complete index of all names and topics in the book but the author does feel that it enables the reader to access most of the subject matter. It does not cover the preface, acknowledgements and appendices.